HOW THE WORLD WORKS

KINGFISHER

First published 2013 by Kingfisher
an imprint of Macmillan Children's Books
a division of Macmillan Publishers Limited
20 New Wharf Road, London N1 9RR
Basingstoke and Oxford
Associated companies throughout the world
www.panmacmillan.com

Created for Kingfisher by Tall Tree Ltd

ISBN 978-0-7534-3637-0

1 3 5 7 9 8 6 4 2
1TR/0713/WKT/UG/128MA

A CIP catalogue record for this book is available from the British Library.

Printed in China

HOW THE WORLD WORKS

CLIVE GIFFORD

KINGFISHER

7-32
EARTH AND SPACE

Earth is a very special place. Our planet is warmed by the energy of the Sun and surrounded by an atmosphere of gas. These conditions have allowed life to develop. Earth's surface is ever-changing – movements of the ground create earthquakes and volcanoes, while storms rage in the atmosphere above. Beyond Earth lie unimaginably vast regions of space containing billions of stars and galaxies.

33-64
PREHISTORIC LIFE

In 1842, British scientist Richard Owen named a group of extinct reptiles dinosauria *from the Greek words for 'terrible' and 'lizard'. Since that time, millions of people have been fascinated with these creatures, which existed on Earth up until around 65 million years ago. Dinosaurs ranged in size from less than 0.7m long up to giant sauropods that were 25m long. Scientists study dinosaur remains in order to learn more about these enigmatic creatures.*

65-96
LIFE

Earth is teeming with a vast range of life, from microscopic, single-celled organisms to gigantic trees, blue whales and elephants. There are believed to be more than eight million different species of living thing. Scientists study the many ways living things find the food and energy they need to grow and stay healthy, as well as how they defend themselves and how they reproduce.

97-128
SCIENCE AND TECHNOLOGY

Science and technology have revolutionized how we live, from powering our homes to saving lives in hospitals and providing communications and entertainment. The results of technology range in size from microscopic electronic components to giant structures such as bridges, tunnels and skyscrapers. Technology has even allowed us to break free from our planet to explore space.

CHAPTER ONE
EARTH AND SPACE

HOW WAS EARTH FORMED?

Earth's story began about 4.6 billion years ago, shortly after the Sun started forming. Dust, ice and rock orbiting the early Sun clumped together in larger and larger lumps that collided with each other, increasing in heat and size.

One of these, Earth, grew in size until it was large enough for its own force of gravity to attract further dust and gas. As the collisions continued, generating huge amounts of heat, the early Earth's surface was repeatedly melted and reshaped. Gradually, minerals rich in iron were drawn towards Earth's centre, forming a large, dense core of iron with lighter rock forming a thick layer, known as the mantle, around the iron. Over many millions of years, the planet cooled, the atmosphere developed and rain fell, eventually forming lakes, seas and oceans.

This image shows what Earth looked like more than a billion years ago. Basins and depressions on the surface were filled with water from rains that lasted thousands of years, creating the early seas and oceans.

Single-celled algae appeared in the sunlit areas of the oceans as early as two billion years ago.

EARTH BIRTH

Earth's formation from a glowing ball of dust and rock to the planet we know today took many hundreds of millions of years. It was almost four billion years before the first multi-celled creatures appeared.

Earth begins to form as matter comes together.

Earth's surface is melted by heat from within as well as by collisions with other objects.

Intense volcanic activity generates gases, forming Earth's early atmosphere.

The planet cools, clouds form and rain falls, producing the early seas.

Movements of parts of the crust, called plates, shape landmasses.

Meteorite impacts create craters and basins on Earth.

Huge volcanic eruptions across the planet create igneous rocks from lava flows, and spew gases into the atmosphere.

Meteorite

Impact crater

MAKING THE MOON

Most astronomers believe that the Moon was formed as a result of a large body colliding with Earth some 4.5 billion years ago. Bombardment by meteorites gave the Moon its cratered surface.

Hot water rises from cracks in the ocean floor called vents.

CANADIAN SHIELD

Snug Harbour on Lake Huron is part of a rocky geological feature known as the Canadian Shield. It features some of the oldest rocks found on Earth, dated to at least 3.8 billion years ago.

Igneous rocks lie on ancient volcanic bedrock.

HOW DO THE CONTINENTS MOVE?

Earth's surface is made of a rocky crust. This crust is not one single piece, but is broken up into a number of giant slabs known as plates, some of which form the world's continents. These sit on top of the mantle – the layer below the surface.

The mantle is about 2,900km thick and ranges in temperature from about 1,000°C to 3,300°C. Heat currents inside the mantle cause the plates above to move by a small amount – between 2cm and 10cm each year. This may not sound like much, but over millions of years it means that the continents travel significant distances. Plates can move apart from one another, or crash together. When they crash, a plate can deform, grind past or slide under another plate. These movements generate earthquakes and volcanic eruptions and create mountain ranges.

DRIFTING APART

About 250 million years ago (mya), all land was part of one supercontinent that scientists call Pangaea. Over time, the supercontinent broke up into smaller continents that began to drift.

1. 225 mya – Pangaea is one supercontinent.

2. 200 mya – Pangaea splits into two sections.

3. 135 mya – the Americas start to move away from Africa and Europe as the Atlantic Ocean widens.

4. Today – Africa is moving north while Asia and North America are moving towards each other.

The continental crust varies in thickness from about 25km to 70km.

Africa lies on the African plate, which for about 100 million years has been moving in a northeasterly direction towards the Eurasian plate. Scientists estimate that it is moving at a rate of about 2.5cm per year.

Oceanic crust

New oceanic crust forms either side of ridge.

Molten rock rises upwards through ridge.

SPREADING CRUST

In the middle of Earth's oceans, new crust forms and spreads between plates. Molten rock rises up through cracks where it cools and hardens in the cold water, creating new oceanic crust. Long chains of undersea mountains lie along these mid-oceanic ridges.

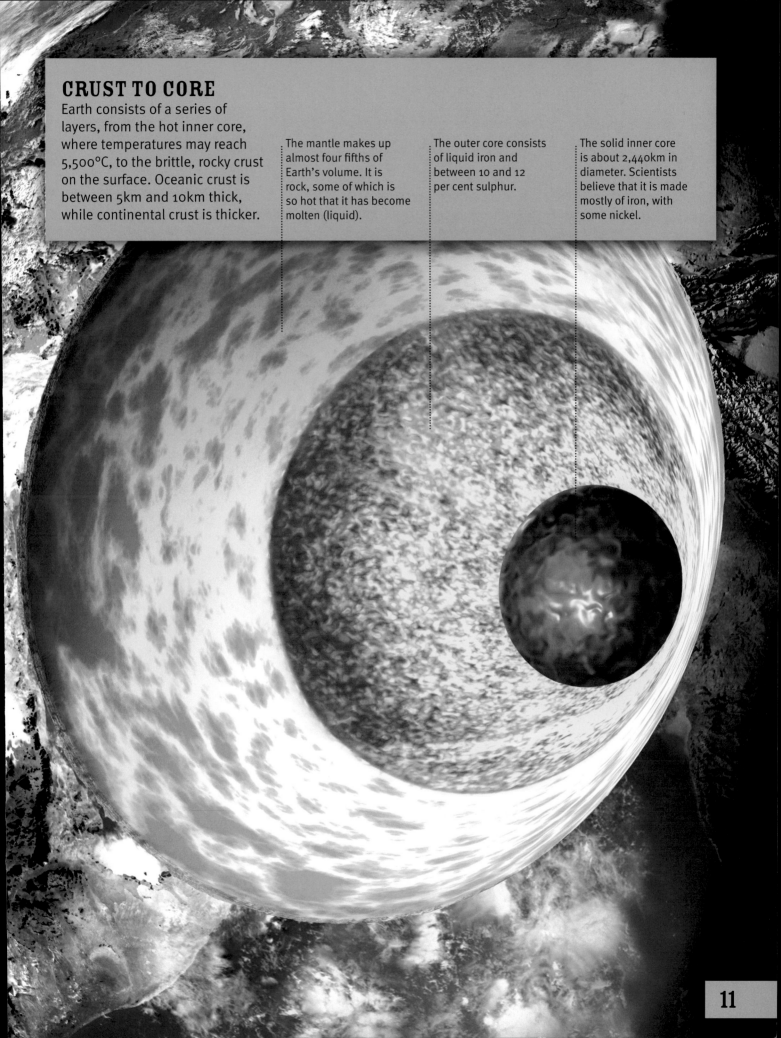

CRUST TO CORE

Earth consists of a series of layers, from the hot inner core, where temperatures may reach 5,500°C, to the brittle, rocky crust on the surface. Oceanic crust is between 5km and 10km thick, while continental crust is thicker.

The mantle makes up almost four fifths of Earth's volume. It is rock, some of which is so hot that it has become molten (liquid).

The outer core consists of liquid iron and between 10 and 12 per cent sulphur.

The solid inner core is about 2,440km in diameter. Scientists believe that it is made mostly of iron, with some nickel.

Energy is released into the ocean, thrusting water upwards and forming tsunami waves.

A continental crust plate is forced upwards by collision with an oceanic plate.

Seismic energy waves radiate out from the earthquake's centre (the focus).

UNDERSEA ACTION

An undersea earthquake often occurs when two plates collide and one plate subducts (slides down) below the other plate. As the energy generated by the quake reaches the seafloor, water is thrust upwards, forming a tsunami.

HOW DO EARTHQUAKES CAUSE TSUNAMIS?

A tsunami is a series of giant waves that can travel quickly across an ocean and strike land with devastating force. Some tsunamis are caused by undersea volcanoes erupting or by an enormous underwater landslide, but most are the result of earthquakes.

An earthquake is a sudden release of built-up energy from Earth's crust. Most earthquakes are caused by the extreme forces and pressures that exist near faults – where two plates grind against each other or collide. As the rocks suddenly release this pressure in the form of energy waves, any water above the earthquake can be jolted upwards with great force, creating powerful waves. Out in the ocean, tsunami waves travel very fast, at speeds of up to 960km/h, but as they approach land, they slow down to 100km/h as the waves grow in height, forming a wall of water that crashes over the land.

A boat lies marooned on land after a powerful 23m-high tsunami struck the coastal town of Funato, Japan, in 2011. The tsunami travelled many kilometres inland, destroying more than 120,000 buildings and causing over 15,000 deaths.

HOW TSUNAMIS FORM

The wavelength (distance between wave crests) of regular ocean waves may be just metres, but the wavelength of tsunamis out in the open ocean can be hundreds of kilometres.

Focus ⋯⋯⋯⋯⋯

⋯⋯⋯⋯⋯ Fault

1. Earthquake occurs, forcing the seafloor and the water above it upwards.

2. Tsunami waves are generated and travel away at high speed.

3. As the waves reach shallower water, the wavelength decreases and the wave height increases.

HOW DO VOLCANOES ERUPT?

Volcanoes are openings in Earth's crust through which molten rock, called magma, along with ash and gases, reach the surface. This process can be a gentle oozing or an explosive, destructive eruption.

Magma is rock deep underground that is heated so much that it flows. Less dense than the surrounding rock, magma may rise and gather in underground pockets known as magma chambers. Sometimes, pressure builds up and forces the magma upwards through cracks in Earth's crust. Magma that reaches the surface is known as lava, and ranges in temperature from 700°C to 1,200°C. The hotter the lava, the thinner and runnier it is. Thick, sticky lava containing a lot of trapped gas can cause violent eruptions. One such eruption happened in 1980 in the United States, when the top 400m of Mount St Helens was blown away.

Magma may also reach the surface through secondary, side vents in the volcano's structure.

This volcano is erupting violently, spewing many tonnes of ash and gas high into the air while red-hot lava runs down its slopes, destroying everything in its path.

Thick, slow-flowing lava travels shorter distances and helps form this steep-sided cone volcano.

LAVA
Here, lava flows into the sea. When lava cools it hardens to form one of a number of types of igneous rock, such as basalt, obsidian or rhyolite.

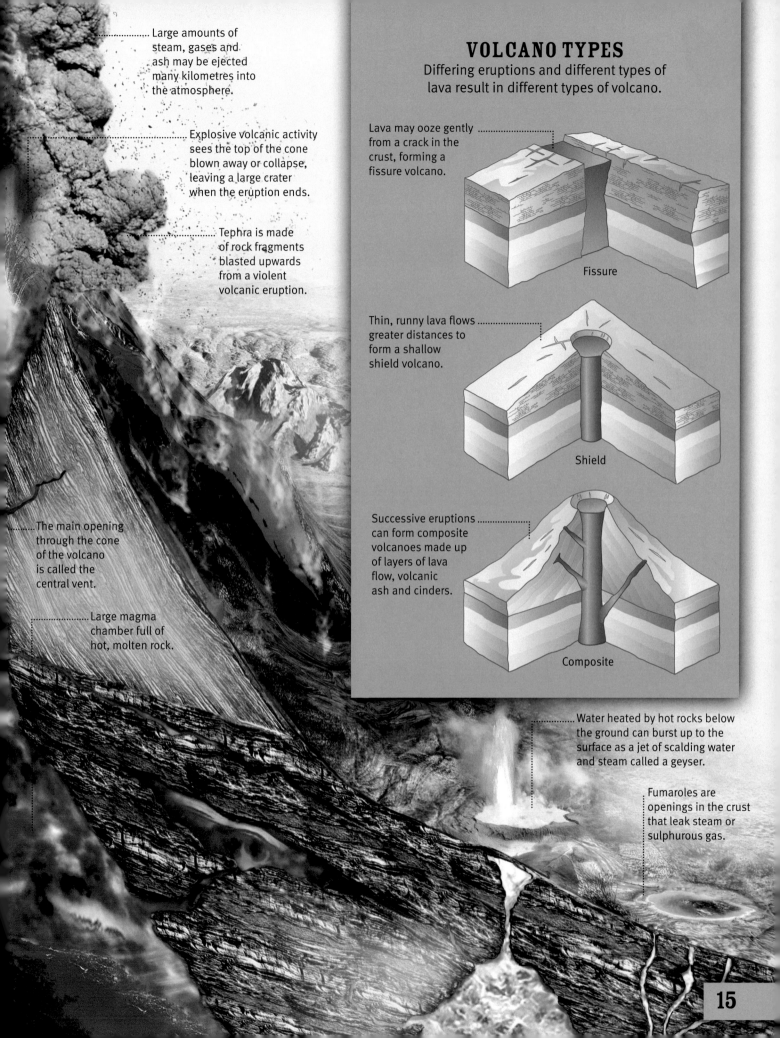

Large amounts of steam, gases and ash may be ejected many kilometres into the atmosphere.

Explosive volcanic activity sees the top of the cone blown away or collapse, leaving a large crater when the eruption ends.

Tephra is made of rock fragments blasted upwards from a violent volcanic eruption.

The main opening through the cone of the volcano is called the central vent.

Large magma chamber full of hot, molten rock.

VOLCANO TYPES
Differing eruptions and different types of lava result in different types of volcano.

Lava may ooze gently from a crack in the crust, forming a fissure volcano.

Fissure

Thin, runny lava flows greater distances to form a shallow shield volcano.

Shield

Successive eruptions can form composite volcanoes made up of layers of lava flow, volcanic ash and cinders.

Composite

Water heated by hot rocks below the ground can burst up to the surface as a jet of scalding water and steam called a geyser.

Fumaroles are openings in the crust that leak steam or sulphurous gas.

HOW DO MOUNTAINS RISE AND FALL?

Mountains are land masses raised steeply above the surrounding land. They are formed in a number of different ways, but mostly through the interaction of the plates in Earth's crust. Eventually, mountains are worn away by erosion.

Earth's crust is made mainly of hard rock, but immense pressures caused by the movements of the plates cause the rock to buckle and bend, or fold over on itself in layers that eventually build up to form large mountain ranges. Examples of these are the Rockies in North America, the Himalayas in Asia and the Andes in South America. Other mountains rise where cracks in Earth's crust allow giant blocks of land to be forced upwards. The Himalayas and other young mountains are still on the rise, but many mountains are decreasing in height as they are worn down by water, wind, icy glaciers and other types of erosion.

This landscape shows the many factors that lead to the formation of mountains – from the slow movement of giant blocks of crust, up and down, to sudden volcanic activity.

Block mountains have a flat top with steep cliffs on either side.

This fault is a significant crack in the Earth's crust.

A block mountain forms where a block of crust is forced upwards by plate movements.

Pressure beneath the surface cracks the crust into blocks. This block has sunk down to form a rift valley.

GLACIATION

Rivers of ice known as glaciers grind and scour rock as they move. Glaciers can shape mountain peaks and create U-shaped valleys such as these, found in the Sherwin Range in the United States.

Glacier has eroded rock into a sharp peak.

Repeated eruptions can result in layers of hardened lava forming mountains.

Sometimes, magma rises and pushes up the land above it – without breaking through to the surface – to form a rounded, dome mountain.

Plates driving together cause rock to lift up, buckle and fold to form fold mountains.

HIMALAYAS

The great Himalaya mountain range of Asia began forming about 55 million years ago when two giant plates in Earth's crust collided.

Rock is folded and faulted to form the giant Himalaya mountain range.

Sediment on ocean floor is pushed upwards by plate movements.

Indo-Australian plate moves northwards, colliding with the Eurasian plate.

Tethys Ocean between the two plates shrinks.

17

HOW DO CLOUDS FORM?

Clouds form through evaporation and condensation. When water is heated, it evaporates and turns into a gas called water vapour. The warm air containing the water vapour is lighter than the liquid water, so it rises. In the sky, the water vapour condenses into a cloud.

As the warm air containing water vapour rises and cools, condensation changes the vapour into millions of small water droplets. This process can be caused by the Sun heating the planet's surface, forcing air to rise over hills and mountains, or when a mass of warm air rises up over a mass of heavier, colder air. As the water droplets collide with each other, they form larger, heavier drops and visible clouds. When the droplets become too heavy for the air to support, they fall as precipitation – rain, snow, hail or sleet (a mixture of rain and snow).

Clouds are a vital part of the water cycle. Driven by the Sun's energy, the cycle is the never-ending sequence of water circulating between the Earth's surface and its atmosphere.

The Sun's heat energy helps water to evaporate from seas, lakes and rivers into the atmosphere.

Water returns to the planet's surface, falling as rain, snow or hail.

Puffy cumulus clouds mostly form when warm air rises and reaches a level of cooler air.

Plants also release water into the atmosphere via the process of transpiration.

Cirrus
Cirrocumulus
Cirrostratus
Altocumulus
Cumulonimbus
Stratus

CLOUD TYPES

Different types of clouds form at different altitudes. These range from ground-hugging stratus clouds to cirrus clouds that form 6,000m or more above the ground.

In very cold air, water droplets freeze into ice crystals, which form snowflakes.

Clouds can travel long distances, moved by winds and air currents.

Snowfall on mountains melts in summer to feed streams and lakes.

Water seeps through cracks in the ground to form a layer of groundwater. The surface of this water is called the water table.

Water runs in streams and rivers from higher altitude down towards sea level.

STORM FORMING

Storm clouds form when rapidly rising warm, moist air reaches cooler parts of the atmosphere.

1. Warm, moist air rises and cools to form cumulus clouds.

2. Rain, snow or hail falls from cumulonimbus clouds, dragging cold air down.

3. An increase of cold air flowing downwards breaks up storm clouds.

19

A number of
thunderstorms
form as clouds.

A large hurricane forms from a series
of thunderstorms generated above a
tropical region of the Atlantic Ocean,
where the hurricane season lasts
from June to November.

Storm grows in
size and, as it
spins, becomes
circular in shape.

HOW DOES A HURRICANE BEGIN?

Hurricanes – or to give them
their scientific name, tropical
cyclones – are giant, spiralling storms
with ferocious wind speeds. They
form out in the oceans and can wreak
havoc and destruction if they travel
over land.

Hurricanes form over the tropical ocean
waters near the equator, where the Sun
evaporates the warm waters quickly, creating
moisture in the air that can form a series of
thunderstorms. These storms merge together,
grow as more heated air moves upwards, and
start to spin when hit by winds, forming a
hurricane. As more hot air is sucked into the
storm, and as cold air is drawn into its centre
from above, the hurricane can reach between
100km and 2,000km in diameter. Its winds swirl
around at speeds as high as 320km/h.

1. Warm air carrying much moisture rises
to form the storm's clouds.

2. Winds force air upwards. This lowers
air pressure, which draws more air upwards
into the storm.

3. Winds outside the hurricane may move
it hundreds of kilometres during the week
or so that it lasts.

TROPICAL CYCLONE CONDITIONS

A hurricane needs ocean water with
temperatures higher than 27°C to provide
the energy and rapid evaporation that
forms its heavy storm clouds.

The eye may be between 15km and 100km wide and is calm, but just outside the eye are a hurricane's most intense winds.

Warm, moist air spirals up around the wall of the hurricane's eye.

Cold, dry air is sucked into the hurricane's low pressure centre called the eye.

Water vapour rising from the ocean forms thick, swirling clouds.

STORM MAP

Tropical cyclones are known as hurricanes in the Caribbean, North Atlantic and northeastern Pacific Ocean, but they are called cyclones in the Indian Ocean and typhoons in the rest of the Pacific.

Hurricanes

Hurricanes

Typhoons

Cyclones

Equator

Cyclones

Cyclones

● Area in which tropical storms form

← Typical path of storms

HURRICANE IRENE

In 2011, Hurricane Irene formed in the Atlantic Ocean. The storm travelled through the Caribbean and up the east coast of the United States, causing more than $20 billion of damage with its 195km/h winds.

HOW DO CORAL REEFS FORM?

Coral reefs may occupy less than one per cent of the world's oceans but they provide incredibly rich habitats for life. These structures are often large, and they are actually formed by tiny marine creatures called coral polyps.

Corals are fixed in one place but use their tentacles to catch prey, which ranges from microscopic plankton to small fish. Scientists have identified more than 1,300 different types of coral. Corals are divided into two groups – soft corals that have a leathery outer surface, and stony corals that create reefs. Stony corals secrete calcium carbonate, or limestone, from their base. These substances form a hard skeleton that offers the corals protection from predators. The skeleton remains after the coral dies. Over time, as coral reproduces and spreads, the skeletons mount up, join other colonies and the coral reef grows.

The Great Barrier Reef off the northeastern coast of Australia is the largest coral reef system in the world. Made up of as many as 400 different corals, its collection of more than 2,500 individual reefs provides a habitat for some 1,500 species of fish.

CORAL FEED

A coral catches some prey by stinging it with its tentacles. However, most of a coral's nutrients come from tiny algae living within the coral's tissue. Coral and algae alike require plenty of sunlight.

A small, neon goby fish is prey for the coral.

Tiny tentacles cover the surface of a brain coral.

Many species of octopus make their home among coral reefs.

Many corals are brightly coloured underwater but lose their colour when they die or are taken out of the water.

The base of the coral is attached to rock on the seafloor.

Some corals have an intricate branching structure like a tree.

REEF TYPES AND ATOLLS

An atoll is formed when a reef continues to grow upwards from a volcanic island that has submerged below sea level. Most atolls are in the Pacific Ocean.

1. Fringing reefs are corals that grow from an island shore into the sea.

2. Barrier reefs form as a volcano sinks. It is separated by a lagoon of open water between the reef and the shore.

Shoreline

Barrier reef

Lagoon

3. An atoll is a reef that forms a circular shape, inside which may be a calm lagoon.

Coral reefs provide homes for 25 per cent of all the world's marine species, including worms, molluscs, crustaceans (such as crabs) and jellyfish.

Delicate corals are at risk from physical impact by humans and larger marine creatures, as well as pollution.

CORAL ISLAND

Found near the Whitsunday Islands in the Great Barrier Reef, this heart-shaped island has been formed by coral growth. It is one of 900 coral islands found in the reef.

HOW ARE DESERTS CREATED?

Deserts are dry regions of land where little water falls from the atmosphere to the ground – usually less than 25cm in total each year. This lack of rain or snowfall occurs for varying reasons in different parts of the world.

Many of the world's deserts, including the Sahara and the Kalahari, are found in subtropical regions where belts of warm, dry, sinking air carry little rainfall. Some deserts are formed because of rain shadows (see right) while continental deserts arise in regions a long way inland and away from the moist air and rainfall of coastal areas. Deserts can also spread because of climate change or human activity. In hot, dry regions near deserts, overgrazing by livestock can clear land of its plant cover. With the loose soil blown or washed away, moisture is not kept in the land and desert conditions can occur.

Desert eagles seek out rodents and other desert creatures to hunt.

A hot desert often experiences baking-hot temperatures during the day but, with few clouds or plants to hold in heat, freezing cold temperatures at night. Deserts pose great survival challenges to the plants and creatures that live there.

Winds carrying sand act as a powerful abrasive, wearing away softer rock to form these unusual pillars.

A cactus stores water in its fleshy stem.

Desert mammals, such as this sand cat, need to shade themselves from the hot Sun.

DIFFERENT DESERTS

Deserts occupy about a third of the planet's land surface but only about a fifth of desert lands are covered in sand. Other deserts have different types of surface.

Snow, ice and, where exposed, bare rock and gravel.

Cold desert

Surface covered in thick sand often blown into dunes.

Sandy desert

Bare rocky plains strewn with stones.

Stony desert

Sand is blown by winds into distinctive sloped mounds called dunes.

Sidewinder snakes, found in North American deserts, slide sideways to glide across the loose sand.

Fennec foxes live in burrows in the Sahara by day and are active during the cooler night.

RAIN SHADOW DESERTS

As full clouds travel over mountains, they cool and release their moisture as rain. The dry air travels over the mountains to the land on the far side, creating a rain shadow desert.

Rising air cools

Dry air travels over mountain carrying little moisture

Prevailing (usual) wind direction

Warm, moist air rises

Water vapour condenses and falls as rain

Rain shadow

The desert cottontail is a rabbit found in the southwestern United States. It requires little water, surviving on the moisture in the plants it eats.

25

HOW DOES THE SUN SHINE?

The Sun is the giant, glowing star at the heart of the Solar System. This glowing ball of gas is so massive that it makes up more than 99.5 per cent of all matter found in the Solar System.

The core of the Sun is a giant nuclear furnace fuelled every second by hundreds of millions of tonnes of hydrogen gas. Nuclear power stations on Earth split atoms to generate large amounts of energy, but the Sun works in a different way. It fuses (joins) the nucleus of hydrogen atoms together to create helium atoms. The vast amounts of energy this generates travel up through the Sun's radiative and convective zones to the surface, which is known as the photosphere. Energy is radiated out through the Solar System by the Sun in the form of light and heat. Light waves from the shining Sun take about eight minutes to reach Earth.

The Sun consists of about 74 per cent hydrogen, 25 per cent helium and small amounts of other elements. Energy is generated in its core and travels through its different layers or zones before being radiated out into the Solar System.

The Sun is so large that more than 1.3 million planet Earths would fit inside it.

NUCLEAR FUSION

Temperatures of about 15 million°C and vast pressures inside the Sun's core force the nuclei of different types of hydrogen atom (deuterium and tritium) to fuse together, creating the nuclei of helium atoms – plus energy.

Tritium atom nucleus contains one proton and two neutrons.

Deuterium atom nucleus contains one proton and one neutron.

Fusion generates a large amount of energy.

A spare neutron from the reaction may react with other atoms.

Fusion reaction joins atoms together to form the nucleus of a helium atom.

Sunspots are cooler areas of the Sun's surface, which appear darker.

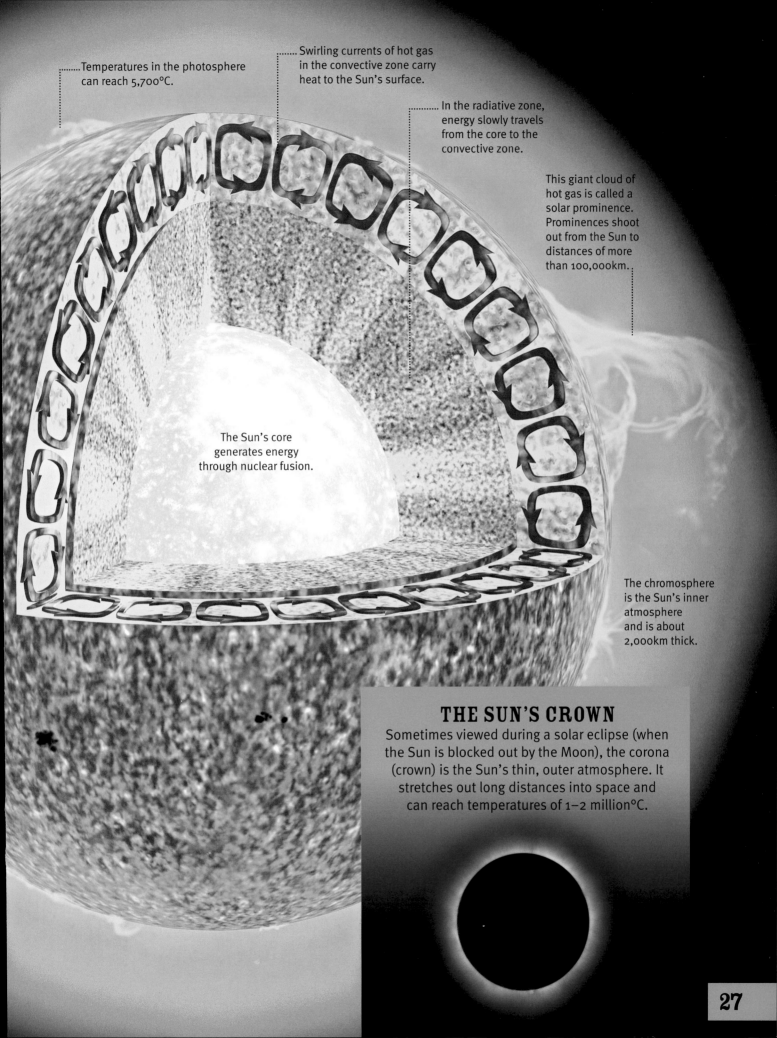

Temperatures in the photosphere can reach 5,700°C.

Swirling currents of hot gas in the convective zone carry heat to the Sun's surface.

In the radiative zone, energy slowly travels from the core to the convective zone.

This giant cloud of hot gas is called a solar prominence. Prominences shoot out from the Sun to distances of more than 100,000km.

The Sun's core generates energy through nuclear fusion.

The chromosphere is the Sun's inner atmosphere and is about 2,000km thick.

THE SUN'S CROWN
Sometimes viewed during a solar eclipse (when the Sun is blocked out by the Moon), the corona (crown) is the Sun's thin, outer atmosphere. It stretches out long distances into space and can reach temperatures of 1–2 million°C.

This pillar of gas is a staggering four light years in height. That is more than 250,000 times the average distance between the Sun and Earth.

These towering pillars of gas and dust are part of the Eagle Nebula. It is located about 7,000 light years from our Solar System.

A star outside the Eagle Nebula is in its main sequence and shines brightly.

Each pillar is mostly made up of hydrogen gas.

This small finger projecting out of the pillar contains dense gas that may form future stars.

STAR BIRTH

Dust and gas is unevenly spread throughout a stellar nursery. This unevenness causes clumps to form, and these eventually become shining stars.

1. Gas and dust are pulled inwards by the force of gravity and clump together.

2. The clumps collapse in on themselves, getting hotter and denser.

3. Pressure and density of the core grow until nuclear fusion begins.

4. Nuclear fusion generates vast amounts of energy, which blasts away surrounding gas and dust.

HOW IS A STAR CREATED?

Stars are giant balls of gas that burn fiercely. Most are born in great stellar 'nurseries' known as nebulas. These vast regions in space are made up of giant clouds of gas and large amounts of dust.

The force of gravity, sometimes caused by an explosion or collision, often triggers star formation. Inside a nebula cloud, gravity makes gas and dust pull together into a clump, which increases in density and temperature. Pressure and heat build at the centre, known as the core, and this generates more gravity and pulls in more and more gas and dust until a protostar – a new star in the making – is formed. If the protostar is large enough, and dense and hot enough, nuclear fusion reactions begin (see pages 26–27) and the star begins to emit huge amounts of energy.

Young stars shine through the gaseous clouds...............

ORION NEBULA

The star nursery nearest to Earth is the Orion Nebula, about 1,400 light years away. It is huge, measuring up to 50 light years across, and is home to thousands of young stars and protostars. On a clear night, it is visible to the naked eye in the constellation Orion.

This black hole formed when a massive star core collapsed in on itself following a supernova explosion. The black hole is so dense and its gravity so strong that everything close by is pulled into it.

DIFFERENT ENDINGS

Stars die in different ways depending on their mass – the amount of matter they contain. Here are three common endings for stars.

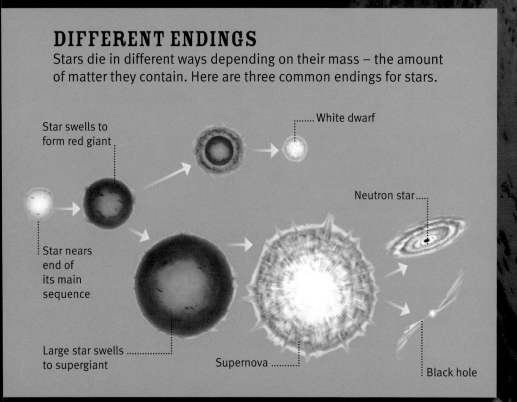

Star swells to form red giant

White dwarf

Neutron star

Star nears end of its main sequence

Large star swells to supergiant

Supernova

Black hole

HOW DO STARS DIE?

Stars begin to die when they run out of the hydrogen that fuels the nuclear reactions in their core. The smallest stars, smaller than the Sun, cool and shrink to form what are known as white dwarfs, which slowly fade. Larger stars end more dramatically.

When an average-sized star, like our Sun, nears the end of its life, it swells in size and casts off many of its outer layers. The shrinking, cooling remains of the star become a white dwarf, which gradually dwindles in energy over millions of years. Massive stars, far bigger than the Sun, die more spectacularly. After swelling to a supergiant, a massive star's core collapses, creating temperatures as high as 10,000 million °C before a supernova explosion blows away the star's outer layers with great force. Sometimes, this leaves behind a small, very dense body called a neutron star.

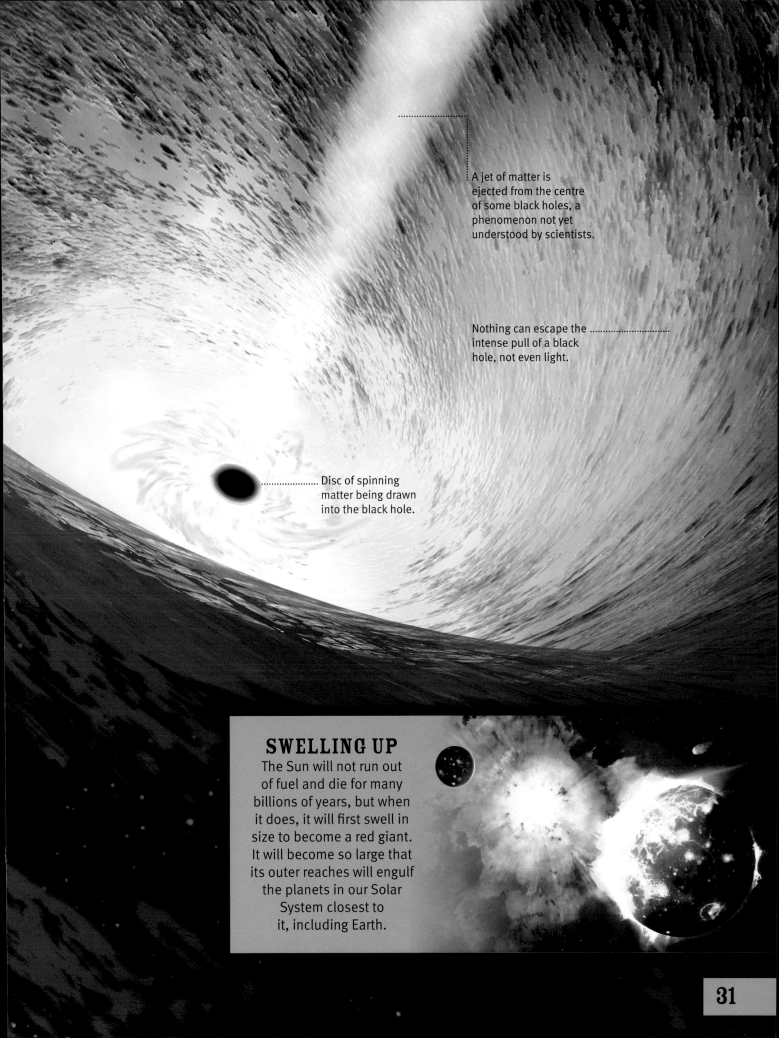

A jet of matter is ejected from the centre of some black holes, a phenomenon not yet understood by scientists.

Nothing can escape the intense pull of a black hole, not even light.

Disc of spinning matter being drawn into the black hole.

SWELLING UP

The Sun will not run out of fuel and die for many billions of years, but when it does, it will first swell in size to become a red giant. It will become so large that its outer reaches will engulf the planets in our Solar System closest to it, including Earth.

EARTH AND SPACE
FIND OUT MORE ABOUT HOW THE WORLD WORKS

WEBSITES TO VISIT

www.learner.org/interactives/dynamicearth/plate.html
See inside our planet and learn about the movement of plates of crust with this informative website.

http://news.bbc.co.uk/1/hi/sci/tech/7533964.stm
Watch animated diagrams showing how volcanoes, tsunamis and earthquakes happen.

www.geology.sdsu.edu/how_volcanoes_work
View images of famous eruptions and read about the different types of volcano found on Earth.

http://earthguide.ucsd.edu/earthguide/diagrams/watercycle/
Watch this clear animation of the water cycle in action.

http://eo.ucar.edu/webweather/cloudhome.html
Spot the different clouds and read more on how clouds form and move.

http://science.howstuffworks.com/nature/natural-disasters/hurricane.htm
Learn more about hurricanes and the destruction they cause.

www.oxfam.org.uk/coolplanet/ontheline/explore/nature/deserts/deserts.htm
Read about all the different deserts of the world, then take a deserts quiz.

www.windows2universe.org/sun/sun.html
See more information on the different zones of the Sun and how they work.

www.esa.int/esaKIDSen/Starsandgalaxies.html
Read about supernovas and other ways stars die at the kids' web pages of the European Space Agency.

http://hubblesite.org/explore_astronomy/black_holes/
Watch animated videos and take a visual journey from Earth to two different black holes at the official website of the Hubble Space Telescope.

BOOKS TO LOOK OUT FOR

• REALLY REALLY BIG QUESTIONS ABOUT SPACE AND TIME by Mark Brake (Kingfisher, 2010)

• EARTH: THE LIFE OF A PLANET by Dr Mike Goldsmith (Kingfisher, 2011)

• THE KINGFISHER SPACE ENCYCLOPEDIA by Dr Mike Goldsmith (Kingfisher, 2012)

• THE ALIEN HUNTER'S HANDBOOK by Mark Brake (Kingfisher, 2012)

CHAPTER TWO
PREHISTORIC LIFE

This *Clevosaurus* is a relative of the tuatara, a reptile found in New Zealand today.

Thecodontosaurus's teeth are adapted to slicing through plant stems and leaves. This early dinosaur is about 1.2–1.5m in length.

A *Thecodontosaurus* (top) grazes on plants during the Triassic period (248–206 million years ago). Its legs are positioned underneath its body and support its weight. Most other reptiles of the time have legs splayed on either side of their bodies.

DINO TIMELINE

The time of the dinosaurs spanned three time periods. Dinosaurs emerged in the Triassic period, and flourished in the Jurassic and Cretaceous periods. There were many types and species. Those shown on the blue lines were lizard-hipped; those on yellow lines were bird-hipped (see box, below).

Tyrannosaurs

Sauropods

Ornithopods

Stegosaurs

Ankylosaurs

Allosaurs

Ceratosaurs

Birds

Dromaeosaurs

Pachycephalosaurs

Ceratopsians

HOW DID DINOSAURS EVOLVE?

Dinosaurs were reptiles that lived on land between 230 million years ago and 65 million years ago. During much of that time, they were the dominant land animals on the planet. They evolved from primitive reptiles, known as archosaurs, that lived before them.

Over time, dinosaurs evolved into many different types, ranging in size from small bird-like creatures to enormous four-legged sauropods, the largest of which measured more than 30m in length and may have weighed as much as 100 tonnes. As some species of dinosaurs died out, new species emerged. So far, scientists have discovered the remains of more than 550 different species of dinosaur. Although the name dinosaur comes from the Greek for 'terrible lizard', many species were gentle plant eaters.

HIP GROUPS

Dinosaurs are grouped by the design of their hip joints. The lizard-hipped ones (saurischians) have a pubis bone that points forwards. The bird-hipped ones (ornithischians) have a backwards-pointing pubis bone.

Bird-hipped

Lizard-hipped

FIRST DINOSAURS

Early dinosaurs such as *Pisanosaurus*, *Eoraptor* and *Hetereodontosaurus* (pictured) flourished about 230 million years ago. *Hetereodontosaurus* was a slim, lizard-hipped dinosaur, about 1.2m long, that ate plants.

Hind (rear) legs supported the dinosaur's weight and allowed it to run.

HOW DID DINOSAUR FOSSILS FORM?

Fossils are the preserved remains or traces of things that lived in the remote past. Most fossils are found in rocks. Much of what we know about dinosaurs comes from the discovery of their fossilized bones or tracks.

A fossil may be a creature's skeleton, or the preserved remains of the food, droppings or tracks the creature left behind (trace fossils). Some fossils are remains preserved in ice. Others are preserved in sticky resin that has hardened to form amber. Most dinosaur fossils, however, are created by layer upon layer of sediment building up over a skeleton that, over time, causes the hard body parts, such as bones and teeth, to solidify in rock layers. Landslides, erosion and movements in Earth's crust may bring these layers to the surface, where they can be discovered by scientists.

These fossilized remains of two dinosaurs dramatically locked in combat were discovered in the Flaming Cliffs region of the Gobi Desert in Mongolia in 1971. The box below, left, shows what occurred.

Protoceratops defends itself.

Velociraptor attacks with its clawed feet.

Velociraptor's front limb catches inside *Protoceratops*'s beak-like mouth.

DINOSAUR DUEL

More than 74 million years ago, a *Velociraptor* attacked a plant-eating *Protoceratops*. The *Protoceratops* fought back, but then a collapsing cliff or a sandstorm covered the creatures in sediment, and their remains began to fossilize.

The long tail of *Protoceratops* is made up of separate bone segments.

The large upper leg bone of *Protoceratops* is preserved in the desert rock.

Velociraptor's lightweight skull is filled with large, sharp teeth. ....

.... Neck bones of *Velociraptor*. The dinosaur was about 1.8–2m long.

.... *Velociraptor*'s leg ended in a foot armed with a large, sickle-shaped claw for slashing prey.

FOSSILIZATION

As the layers of sediment on top of a dinosaur skeleton mount, pressure builds and the sediment hardens. Minerals from the sediment fill the skeleton, preserving the shape of the bones – which over time have become rock.

1. Dinosaur dies and soft body parts begin to decompose (rot away).

2. Remains are covered in layers of sand, mud or other sediment.

3. Fossilization occurs as layers of sediment harden into rock.

4. Rock layers above are eroded to bring fossil skeleton to the surface.

SEALED IN CAVES

Some fossil deposits of dinosaurs have been found surrounded by strata (layers) of much earlier rock. This is because the dinosaur may have fallen or been washed away into deep caves.

1. Dinosaur grazes on plants close to limestone depressions and caves.

2. Dinosaur dies and its body is washed away by rains or floods into the cave.

3. Layers of sediment build up over the bones to create fossils (see box above).

HOW DO WE KNOW ABOUT DINOSAURS?

The fossil record has taught us much about the size, structure and habits of dinosaurs. Making new fossil discoveries, and investigating further those already made, helps experts to learn more about how dinosaurs lived and died.

Palaeontology is the scientific study of prehistoric life. It includes a range of different subjects, from geology to biology and computer science. Some palaeontologists specialize in studying one particular dinosaur or one fossil type, such as teeth or fossilized plants. Others concentrate on seeking out fossil beds that may yield important new finds. Fossils have to be identified and some experts use scanning microscopes and other new technologies to examine them in great detail. Wear marks on teeth and jaw bones, for example, can provide important information about how and what a dinosaur ate.

In 1947, US palaeontologist Edwin H Colbert discovered more than 100 *Coelophysis* skeletons at Ghost Ranch in New Mexico, USA. These early dinosaurs lived about 210 million years ago. The group may have been killed suddenly by a flash flood.

Skull has large eye sockets, so scientists think that *Coelophysis* had good eyesight. ....

A large adult *Coelophysis* stood about 1m tall at the hip. ....

Small, pointed head with mouth containing about 80 small, sharp teeth for tearing at flesh. ....

DIGGING DEEP
Palaeontologists unearth the fossilized skeleton of an *Edmontosaurus* at Hell Creek in North Dakota, USA. The bones have to be cleaned carefully, catalogued and then compared with others to confirm the dinosaur type.

Mandible (lower jaw)

Long neck made of many individual vertebrae bones.

Three-toed foot

BONE JIGSAW

Skeletons are rarely found whole, so much detective work has to be done to piece the parts together. Sometimes 'complete' skeletons on display in museums use bones from different skeletons.

Long tail keeps the dinosaur balanced and agile as it runs.

Large leg bones are hollow, for lightness and speed.

3D MODELLING

Some scientists use computers to create 3D models of dinosaur skeletons. These help us to study dinosaur body parts and see how they may have moved and worked.

HOW DID MARINE REPTILES LIVE DURING THE DINOSAUR AGE?

Dinosaurs were reptiles that lived on land, although occasionally some did venture into water. Marine reptiles existed at the same time as the dinosaurs and lived their whole lives in the seas and oceans.

The waters of Earth's prehistoric seas were teeming with fish, squid-like animals and creatures with hard shells such as ammonites. Large marine reptiles such as plesiosaurs, nathosaurs and ichthyosaurs would catch these animals in powerful jaws, crushing the shells and spines and swallowing the prey whole. Some of these predators became prey themselves for the largest, most ferocious marine reptiles such as *Liopleurodon*. Marine reptiles did not have gills like fish so they needed to surface to breathe air.

More than 150 million years ago, plesiosaurs swam the Jurassic seas in search of prey. These large marine reptiles had broad, shallow bodies with long necks, and typically grew to about 3.5m in length.

Plesiosaurs 'fly' through the water by flapping their two pairs of flippers alternately.

ICHTHYOSAURS

These shark-like marine reptiles had long, slim jaws lined with many sharp teeth for catching fish and molluscs. Large eyes may have helped them to hunt in murky waters. One species of ichthyosaur, *Temnodonotosaurus*, had gigantic eyes – each at least 20cm wide.

A long, flexible spine ended in a gristly tail that would beat back and forth to move through water.

Small hind fins may have helped to keep the reptile balanced in the water.

Large eye socket

Elasmosaurus was a marine reptile that lived about 80 million years ago, mostly near the water's surface. It possessed the longest neck of any known marine reptile. The neck measured between 5m and 6.5m long and was made up of more than 70 vertebrae.

Nostrils on top of head to breathe air when surfacing.

Long, flexible neck swings back and forth through shoals of fish when hunting.

Sharp, cone-shaped teeth line the jaw, allowing plesiosaurs to rip and tear prey.

Powerful jaw muscles generated huge crushing forces.

PLIOSAURS

Thrust upwards by the force of its muscular flippers, a pliosaur catches an ichthyosaur in its fearsome jaws. One of the largest pliosaur skulls ever found – off the coast of Dorset, England, in 2008 – measured 2.4m in length.

HOW DID PREHISTORIC REPTILES FLY?

Many species of flying reptiles, known as pterosaurs, soared through the skies in prehistoric times. Close relatives of dinosaurs, they possessed lightweight bodies and large wings made of living tissue rather than feathers.

Pterosaurs may have been clumsy on land, walking on all fours and using the claws on their wings to crawl. They were more agile in the air, using their large wings to glide on air currents and their keen eyesight and long beaks to seek out food to catch and eat. Some species of pterosaur had an area of tissue between their rear legs, which formed an extra wing called an uropatagium.

Three different species of pterosaur glide above the Solnhofen lagoon. This is now a region in southern Germany, an area rich in pterosaur fossils.

Large eye is used for detecting prey.

Rhamphorhynchus's arm ends in four finger-like digits. The first three form a claw while the very long fourth digit extends along the front edge of the wing.

A *Ctenochasma* flies low to the ground. Adult *Ctenochasma* had as many as 400 teeth in their long beaks.

IN FLIGHT

Scientists are still learning about pterosaurs and flight. This model shows how a large pterosaur may have flown. Its giant wings are attached to its arms and body and are made of thin layers of a strong, leathery membrane.

1. The pterosaur keeps its wings largely still as it soars on warm, rising air.

2. Powerful muscles attached to its body pull its arms and wings downwards and then push upwards.

3. As the wings move up and down, their curve may alter in shape, generating some extra lift.

A flock of *Pterodactylus* swoops over coastal waters seeking fish to catch and eat.

Large wing membrane contains fibres to stiffen them, muscles and blood vessels.

Long tail ends in a diamond-shaped vane that provides stabilization during flight.

GIANT PTEROSAUR

The largest known species of flying reptile was *Quetzalcoatlus northropi*. Fossil remains reveal that it had a gigantic wingspan of 11–12m – as large as a light aircraft. This replica of a *Quetzalcoatlus* skeleton is displayed in a museum in Australia.

Neck is almost 3m long and made up of just seven vertebrae.

Rear legs trail behind pterosaur's body and wings.

HOW DID DINOSAURS WALK AND RUN?

Dinosaurs varied greatly in size and weight but they all relied on large muscles attached to their leg and hip bones for movement. Stretches of tough, fibrous tissue called tendons connected the muscles to the bones. The muscles contracted and relaxed to move their legs.

Some dinosaurs were bipeds, meaning that they walked on two legs. Others, like *Iguanadon*, grazed on all four legs but ran on their stronger back two legs. Smaller bipeds, such as *Gallimimus* and *Eoraptor*, may have been able to sprint at 40–50km/h or faster. However, the giant four-legged sauropods, such as *Apatosaurus* and *Diplodocus*, moved far more slowly. Fossilized footprints show that they would stride forwards with one front leg and a rear leg on the opposite side, then take their next step with their other two legs moving forwards.

Eoraptor, an early dinosaur, runs on two legs to catch a small lizard. Relatively small at 1m long, and nimble, *Eoraptor* uses its speed both to hunt and to outrun other predators.

Eoraptor is an omnivore – it eats both animals and plants.

Good eyesight allows *Eoraptor* to hunt small, fast-moving prey.

Jaw is fitted with both carnivore and herbivore types of teeth – some sharp for slicing; some blunt for grinding.

BONE DETECTIVES

Fossilized skeletons offer palaeontologists important clues about how dinosaurs may have moved. These are often compared with the movements of creatures alive today that have similar skeletons.

Tail may have been used to help dinosaur balance as it changed direction.

Leg structure enables scientists to guess the length of its stride.

Foot design shows that this dinosaur is a digitigrade – a creature that runs on its toes.

Heavy tail helped to balance the weight of the dinosaur's head.

FAST PREDATOR

A large, predatory dinosaur from Mongolia, *Tarbosaurus* moved quickly over short distances and used its enormous, 1.3m-long head as a battering ram when attacking prey.

Small arms for grappling with prey.

Large, powerful rear legs. *Tarbosaurus* stood about 3.8m tall at its hips.

Hip joint connects upper leg bone to dinosaur's spine.

Tail bones

Tail acts as a counterweight balancing the forward tilt of *Eoraptor*'s neck and body.

Strong upper leg and hip muscles generate the power for quick movement.

TRACKS

Series of fossilized footprints have left behind 'dino highways' for palaeontologists to study. These can reveal much about different dinosaurs' running speeds, stride lengths and movement.

Gallimimus may have sprinted at speeds of up to 50km/h.

Apatosaurus covered about 5m each time one of its legs took a stride.

Rear legs of *Dryosaurus* left prints in drying mud.

Eoraptor walks and runs on its front three toes.

Hinge joint allows dinosaur to tilt its foot up or down.

SAUROPODS IN SCALE

Sauropods varied greatly in size. The smallest were 6–7m long; the largest up to 50–60m long. Here are six giant sauropod species.

1. *Supersaurus*
2. *Bruhathkayosaurus*
3. *Diplodocus*
4. *Amphicoelias*
5. *Sauroposeidon*
6. *Argentinosaurus*

Brachiosaur's chisel-shaped teeth strip branches of leaves.

About 160 million years ago, herds of brachiosaurs crash through foliage, feeding on trees. With long front legs, these animals stand 12m tall and can strip leaves off trees taller than other plant-eaters.

LIVING TOGETHER

Scientists believe that different types of sauropod grazed together in the same areas. Taller sauropods feasted on leaves high up in the treetops, leaving lower-lying trees and plants for shorter sauropods to eat.

Diplodocus grew to 30m in length.

An average *Camarasaurus* was 15m long.

A younger brachiosaur rears up to reach araucaria tree leaves.

HOW DID SAUROPODS SURVIVE?

Sauropods were the largest animals ever to have walked the Earth. The heaviest weighed more than 100 tonnes. Equipped with four stout legs, a long neck and long tail, these plant-eating giants had to graze constantly in order to survive.

Sauropods' sheer size made them hard to attack. Most had a small head perched on a long neck to give them a wide feeding range from one position. Food was not chewed but swallowed and digested in the body with the help of swallowed stones to pulp the food. Despite their slow movement and lack of defences, sauropods flourished. Their fossils have been found on every continent except Antarctica.

Neck skeleton is made up of a series of vertebrae bones.

Gizzard contains swallowed stones that pulp and grind up swallowed food.

Huge thigh bones help support the dinosaur's weight of about 20 tonnes.

Large lungs help fill sauropod's blood with oxygen.

SAUROPOD STRUCTURE

Because so little of a dinosaur's soft tissue is ever fossilized, scientists make guesses about what the inside of a sauropod looked like. This diagram shows a *Rapetosaurus*, one of a group of titanosaurus sauropods that were among the last to exist – up until about 65 million years ago.

Giant stomach where plants are partially digested.

PROTECTIVE CIRCLE

Adult *Triceratops* were hefty, four-legged dinosaurs, measuring about 8–9m in length. They may have used their considerable bulk to protect the herd's young from an attack by forming a defensive circle, with the adults' horned heads pointing outwards.

HOW DID DINOSAURS LIVE TOGETHER IN HERDS?

Large numbers of the same species of dinosaur have been found together in fossil sites known as bonebeds. A herd of styracosaurs was found in a bonebed in Arizona, USA, for example. Living in a large, moving herd made it harder for predators to single out an individual.

Other evidence for dinosaur herds comes from large groups of fossil footprints known as trackways, and from the discovery of nesting sites with many fossilized eggs. Some herds may have been temporary, such as when dinosaurs gathered at a water hole, but many dinosaurs lived in herds all their lives. Herds provided partners to mate with, help with raising young, and offered protection from attack by predators.

A herd of *Triceratops* roams the late Cretaceous landscape during the breeding season. Two large males fight, competing for females. They crash their enormous, bone-frilled heads and gore each other with their horns until one submits.

Horns measure up to 1m in length.

PACK SAFETY

This picture shows a herd of *Iguanodon* fleeing an attack from the fast, predatory dinosaur *Deinonychus*. Adult *Iguanodon* positioned themselves at the front and rear of the group to protect their young in the middle of the pack.

Adult *Iguanodon* running with head held low.

Young *Iguanodon* running alongside the adults.

49

SUPER SPRINTER

Struthiomimus may have been a predator, eating lizards as well as plants. When threatened with attack from larger predators, however, its powerful legs helped it to sprint to safety at speeds of 50km/h or more.

HOW DID DINOSAURS DEFEND THEMSELVES?

Some dinosaurs escaped predators by camouflaging themselves, or by using their speed to evade a predator. Others possessed heavy body armour or body parts specialized to fend off attacks.

We do not know how dinosaur skin was coloured, but it is likely that some dinosaurs could conceal themselves in forests or undergrowth using their skin colour as camouflage. Others did not need camouflage because they had thick armour for protection. *Protoceratops* and *Triceratops* had a bony frill around their head that helped to protect their neck from attack. Others, such as *Ankylosaurus*, had a body covered in tough plates, making them hard to injure. Attacked dinosaurs may have used the claws on their feet to fight back or they may have lashed out with their tail.

Bony plates are covered in horny knobs and spikes called osteoderms.................

DINO ARMOUR

Stegosaurus was a heavily built dinosaur living about 150 million years ago. The series of large, bony plates running along its back may have helped it to keep cool, but may also have protected it from attack by making it look larger than it really was.

Largest bony plates were about 60cm high and 60cm wide.

Strong tail armed with four spikes was a powerful defensive weapon.

Ankylosaurus's club may have weighed more than 50kg.

A large meat-eater, *Albertosaurus*, attacks a plant-eater, *Ankylosaurus*, which fights back using its armoured tail. The tail ends in a heavy club made of bone. A powerful swing could bash the attacker's body with enough force to break bones.

HAND AND FOOT SPURS

Some species of dinosaur had sharp spikes or horns on their feet known as spurs. These may have been used to stab or slash an enemy when attacked. This *Iguanodon* had a large, pointed spike in the thumb position on each hand.

HOW DID TYRANNOSAURS HUNT AND KILL PREY?

Tyrannosaurus rex is the most famous dinosaur of all. This fearsome meat-eater was one of the largest land carnivores, growing up to 12.5m long and weighing 5–7 tonnes. It was also one of the last dinosaurs to become extinct.

No one is certain whether this dinosaur hunted and killed its own food or whether it was a scavenger, seeking prey that was already dead. Its arms, though small, may have been very muscular, and its hands – ending in two sharp claws – may have helped it to grip prey at close quarters. Palaeontologists believe that the dinosaur had a strong sense of smell, perfect for hunting, but also suitable for seeking out dead, rotting carcasses long distances away.

IN FOR THE KILL

This sequence shows one way in which *Tyrannosaurus rex* may have attacked and killed a duck-billed dinosaur named *Anatotitan*.

1. *T-rex* stalks its prey, a herd of *Anatotitan* that is trapped in a forest clearing.

2. One animal is singled out and circled before *T-rex* lunges and clamps its massive jaws on the prey's neck.

3. Loss of blood or a crushed windpipe causes *Anatotitan* to collapse.

.... Jaw and neck muscles were so strong that this dinosaur could kill by shaking its victims apart.

BITE AND TEAR

Here, a *T-rex* is shown feasting on its prey. A blunt snout, powerful jaws and 30cm-long teeth enabled it to slice and tear away flesh, possibly as much as 75kg of meat in a single bite.

.... Duck-billed *Corythosaurus* is a plant-eater that measures up to 10m long.

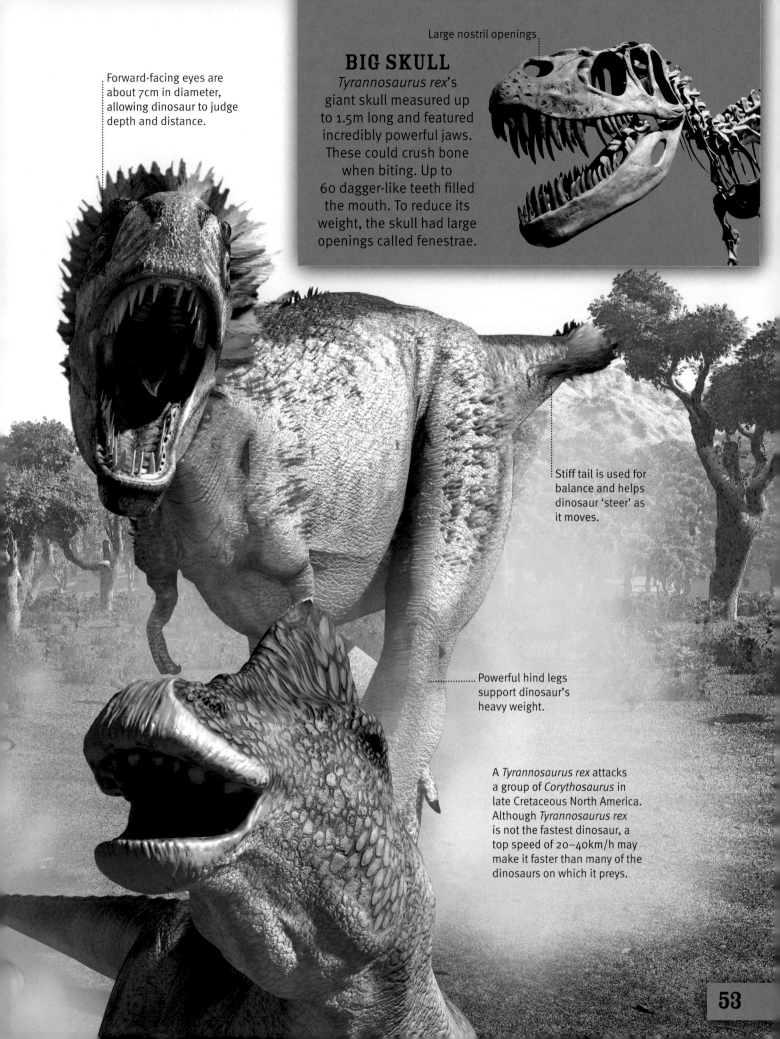

Forward-facing eyes are about 7cm in diameter, allowing dinosaur to judge depth and distance.

Large nostril openings

BIG SKULL
Tyrannosaurus rex's giant skull measured up to 1.5m long and featured incredibly powerful jaws. These could crush bone when biting. Up to 60 dagger-like teeth filled the mouth. To reduce its weight, the skull had large openings called fenestrae.

Stiff tail is used for balance and helps dinosaur 'steer' as it moves.

Powerful hind legs support dinosaur's heavy weight.

A *Tyrannosaurus rex* attacks a group of *Corythosaurus* in late Cretaceous North America. Although *Tyrannosaurus rex* is not the fastest dinosaur, a top speed of 20–40km/h may make it faster than many of the dinosaurs on which it preys.

HOW DID DINOSAURS HUNT IN PACKS?

Some dinosaurs may have worked together in packs to bring down and kill much larger prey. Evidence for packs comes from the numbers of fossils, found together, of the same species of small, predatory dinosaurs.

While some dinosaurs had good defences, such as a spiked tail or horn, they could repel only one or two predators at the same time. A pack of predators could overwhelm even the toughest dinosaur, weakening it with attack after attack until it fell. Smaller predators such as *Deinonychus* and *Velociraptor* may have worked together in intelligent groups, communicating with one another as they stalked their prey. *Velociraptor* may have taken turns to leap on the back of their prey, biting and slashing with their claws.

This giant *Argentinosaurus* is too large for a single *Giganotosaurus* to bring down. But working together as a pack, a group of *Giganotosaurus* can attack the sauropod repeatedly. Soon it collapses from exhaustion, injury and blood loss.

Giganotosaurus may have weighed 8–9 tonnes – more than a *Tyrannosaurus rex*.

LIGHTWEIGHT KILLER
Velociraptor's skull was about 25cm long. It was light in weight and had serrated teeth suited to tearing small amounts of flesh. *Velociraptor* was too small to bring down large prey by itself, so scientists believe this dinosaur often hunted in packs.

Attacker takes a bite while clawing its victim's flank with its sharp claws.

Argentinosaurus measures more than 25m in length and weighs 60–75 tonnes.

PACK ATTACK

A group of *Deinonychus* are shown here savaging a *Tenontosaurus* in a forest during the Cretaceous period. Two jumped on the animal's back while a third attacked its neck. *Deinonychus* had huge claws on its second toes. It used these to slash and tear its prey.

Giganotosaurus attacks the neck area, aiming to cut major arteries.

HOW DID DINOSAURS SEE, SMELL, TASTE AND HEAR?

Studying dinosaurs' senses is difficult because so little evidence of their eyes and other sense organs remains. However, experts believe that dinosaurs were equipped with sense organs remarkably similar to those found in animals today.

Vision may have been many dinosaurs' most important sense. Some would have had a wide field of vision that allowed them to see in almost all directions without moving their head – vital for spotting signs of danger. Others, particularly predators, had binocular vision in which the eyes' field of vision overlapped. This enabled them to judge distances to objects accurately. The sense of smell was important, too, for sniffing out prey, particular plants to eat or a mate to breed with. Taste was probably the weakest of most dinosaurs' senses.

HIGH AND LOW

Different types of dinosaurs could probably hear different frequencies of sounds. This is similar to the way large modern birds can hear lower-pitched sounds better than small birds, which are better at hearing higher-pitched sounds.

Hearing detects low-pitched thuds of a large dinosaur's footsteps as it approaches.

Head rears up so that eyes can search for signs of approaching danger.

Pupil of eye is slit-shaped for viewing in bright sunlight. In the dark, it opens wide.

FIELD OF VIEW

Dinosaurs with forward-facing eyes, such as *Tyrannosaurus rex*, combined excellent eyesight with a strong sense of smell. But most plant-eating dinosaurs had eyes on the sides of the head, giving them good all-round views.

Troodon has eyes on side of head.

Wide field of vision with each eye.

Narrow area where the two eyes can produce 3D views.

Olfactory lobes at the front of the brain are responsible for *Troodon*'s sense of smell.

In the ears, fluid-filled tubes called semicircular canals provide a sense of balance.

Large brain receives signals from all sense organs and processes them intelligently.

Large eye can see in low light conditions, such as dawn, dusk and even at night.

Nostrils close in a sandstorm but open to let air travel through and into the mouth.

A *Troodon* carries a small lizard it has caught in its mouth. This 2m-long meat-eater from North America had a larger than average brain for its size, so many dinosaur experts believe it was especially skilled at processing signals from its senses, particularly its eyes.

57

Air circulates around crest's hollow tubes.

CREST CALLS

An examination of hadrosaur skull fossils shows how their nostrils ran up into their crest. Air forced around a hadrosaur's crest and out the nostrils would have been amplified (made louder), similar to the way in which sound is produced in a trombone.

Air forced out through the nostrils.

Tail feathers fanned out make a display.

MICRORAPTOR

These small *Microraptor* dinosaurs from China lived about 120 million years ago. Their fossils were found to have feathers on the arms, legs and tail. These may have been fluffed out at times of danger as a warning to others, or displayed to protect territory, or used to attract a mate, or all of these things.

WHIP CRACKING

Diplodocus had a very long tail made up of more than 70 bony vertebrae, which it may have cracked like a whip to make an extremely loud sound. This may have scared off predators, and helped *Diplodocus* keep in contact with its herd over long distances.

Tail tapers so that it was slender along much of its length.

Crest made of bone with hollow passages throughout.

HOW DID DINOSAURS COMMUNICATE?

The dinosaur age was far from silent. The thuds of giant footsteps and the cries and crashes of battling dinosaurs may have mixed with the roars and mating calls of others. Dinosaurs may have also used visual signals to communicate.

We cannot be certain what dinosaurs sounded like, but we can be fairly sure that they made noises. Judging by the size of some dinosaurs' lungs, many of these noises may have been extremely loud. Certain duck-billed dinosaurs, known as hadrosaurs, all had large, bony crests on the top of their head through which air may have circulated to produce loud, trumpeting sounds. Dinosaurs may also have used visual displays or body language – such as foot stamping, rearing up or shaking their head when trying to attract a mate or defend territory from others in the herd.

Parasaurolophus was a hadrosaur with an enormous head crest that curved backwards from its head. This may have allowed it to produce a bellow loud enough to be heard over great distances.

HOW WERE DINOSAURS BORN?

Major fossil finds show that dinosaurs laid eggs, just as birds, fish and reptiles do today. Fossilized dinosaur eggs have been found in more than 200 sites throughout the world. Most are around 10–20cm long.

The egg, sometimes laid in nests, provided a food source for the dinosaur embryo as it developed. The shell protected the embryo, and would be broken by the baby dinosaur's beak or claws when it was ready to hatch. Some newly hatched dinosaurs were able to walk and eat as soon as they were born. Other species needed looking after. Worn teeth of fossilized baby dinosaurs, found in nests, show that they were brought food – small leaves, seeds and berries – by their parents, who would also have protected them from small, fast predators.

A group of *Maiasaura* rear their young. Babies hatch from eggs laid in circular nests. As many as 40 eggs are laid in a single nest. *Maiasaura* nests found in Montana, USA, were repaired, suggesting that the dinosaurs returned to the same nesting sites to lay their eggs.

MOTHER AND YOUNG

A group of infant dinosaurs, no more than a year old, are shown here huddling around their mother. Among the fossil remains of dinosaurs, including *Psittacosaurus* and *Maiasaura*, young dinosaurs have been found close to adults that were probably their parents.

An infant *Maiasaura* grows fast, probably doubling its size in less than two months.

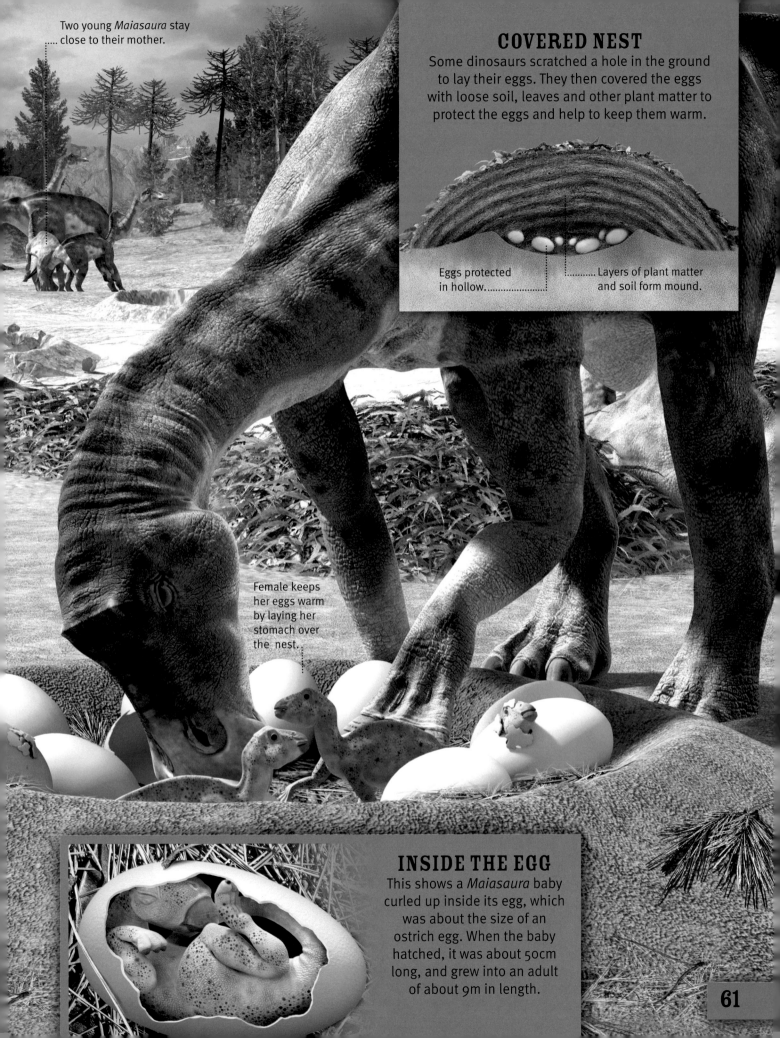

Two young *Maiasaura* stay close to their mother.

COVERED NEST

Some dinosaurs scratched a hole in the ground to lay their eggs. They then covered the eggs with loose soil, leaves and other plant matter to protect the eggs and help to keep them warm.

Eggs protected in hollow.

Layers of plant matter and soil form mound.

Female keeps her eggs warm by laying her stomach over the nest.

INSIDE THE EGG

This shows a *Maiasaura* baby curled up inside its egg, which was about the size of an ostrich egg. When the baby hatched, it was about 50cm long, and grew into an adult of about 9m in length.

IMPACT SITE

A rocky object from space struck Earth in the Yucatán Peninsula of present-day Mexico. The resulting Chicxulub crater, almost 200km in diameter, was discovered only in the 1970s, buried under new rocks formed since the impact.

Meteorite was destroyed upon impact.

HOW DID THE DINOSAURS DIE OUT?

After flourishing for more than 160 million years, dinosaurs, large marine reptiles and many other creatures were suddenly wiped out. Most scientists think that this mass extinction was caused by a massive meteorite impact.

About 65.5 million years ago, a large meteorite, at least 10–16km in diameter, is thought to have struck Earth. The resulting blast, more powerful than two million atomic bombs, generated intense heat, giant tsunami waves and vast clouds of dust. These clouds blotted out sunlight, plunging the world into cold and darkness, possibly for many years. Dinosaurs were unable to survive the devastation and the floods or the extreme change in climate and lack of food that followed, as many plant species were wiped out, too. However, some creatures did survive, including early birds, many insects and small mammal species.

Alamosaurus is one of the last sauropods.

SURVIVOR

Cimolestes was a small species of mammal that existed both before and after the mass extinction of dinosaurs. Among other survivors were many species of insect, turtles and crocodiles.

Pointed mouth evolved for eating insects.

NEW SPECIES

Over time, new species of creatures evolved. Nimravidae, a species of sabre-toothed cat, flourished more than 20 million years after the dinosaurs died out. A large, predatory mammal, it too became extinct about seven million years ago.

Large dinosaurs, such as this *Tyrannosaurus rex*, will be wiped out.

Dinosaurs flee in terror from the intense heat and dust caused by the meteorite impact. Species that cannot cope with the new climate conditions will quickly become extinct.

Triceratops is among the last of the ceratopsians.

PREHISTORIC LIFE
FIND OUT MORE ABOUT HOW THE WORLD WORKS

WEBSITES TO VISIT

www.kidsdinos.com/palaeontology-article.php
Learn more about palaeontology and the tools palaeontologists use at this colourful website.

www.dinohunters.com/index.htm
Find out who discovered which dinosaurs first and read short profiles of famous fossil finders, including Mary Anning and Gideon Mantell.

www.nhm.ac.uk/nature-online/life/dinosaurs-other-extinct-creatures/dino-directory/index.html
Check out the details of more than 300 dinosaur species at this Dino Directory created by the Natural History Museum, London.

http://dsc.discovery.com/dinosaurs/
Here you will find key facts and images on a wide range of different dinosaurs.

www.dinosaurcentral.com/fieldguide.php
Explore a database of more than 150 different species of dinosaur.

www.newscientist.com/article/dn9919-instant-expert-dinosaurs.html
Check out New Scientist *magazine's introductory guide to dinosaurs and how they lived. The web pages also include the latest news on dinosaur finds.*

www.ucmp.berkeley.edu/diapsids/saurischia/tyrannosauridae.html
Learn more about Tyrannosaurus rex *and see how a skeleton is prepared for display.*

www.discoveringfossils.co.uk/whatisafossil.htm
Read more about how fossils are made and view many famous fossil-hunting sites around Britain in this website's resources section.

www.plesiosauria.com/index.php
Learn about different plesiosaur species and how they lived and moved at the website of marine reptile researcher Dr Adam Stuart Smith.

http://science.nationalgeographic.com/science/prehistoric-world/mass-extinction/
Read about mass extinctions in Earth's past, then view the galleries of dinosaurs and fossils found on the National Geographic website.

BOOKS TO LOOK OUT FOR

• THE KINGFISHER DINOSAUR ENCYCLOPEDIA by Professor Mike Benton (Kingfisher, 2009)
• NAVIGATORS: DINOSAURS by David Burnie (Kingfisher, 2010)
• EVERYTHING YOU NEED TO KNOW ABOUT DINOSAURS by Dougal Dixon (Kingfisher, 2012)

CHAPTER THREE
LIFE

Some rainforest trees grow to great heights in order to compete for light.

PHOTOSYNTHESIS

Chloroplasts contain the substance chlorophyll, which absorbs energy from sunlight. This produces a chemical reaction with water (drawn up by the plant's roots) and carbon dioxide gas (taken in from the air) to produce oxygen and glucose.

Sunlight reaches the leaf, where chlorophyll aborbs the light's energy.

Carbon dioxide is absorbed by the leaves through tiny pores called stoma.

Oxygen is released from leaves through the stoma.

Water, carbon dioxide and the energy from sunlight react inside chloroplasts to generate sugars and oxygen.

Glucose is either moved around the plant or stored as food.

HOW DO PLANTS GROW?

Plants need sunlight, water, air and soil to grow. Most species of plants make their food for growth through a process known as photosynthesis. This takes place in chloroplasts (specialized cells) inside the plant's leaves.

Photosynthesis creates energy-rich sugars that are transported around the plant as food or are made into more complex chemicals and stored inside the plant. These chemicals include cellulose, which is used to build new cell walls when the plant's cells grow and divide as it grows bigger. If a young plant continues to get the right nutrients and the right conditions for it to photosynthesize, it will grow into a mature plant. A few plants do not get everything they need from photosynthesis or from the soil. Some, such as the Venus fly trap and bladderworts, digest insects to gain nutrients. Others, such as ivy and orchids, are parasites – they grow upon, and take nutrients from, other plants.

A tropical rainforest is dense with trees and plant life, most seeking out sunlight to help fuel their growth. Below the main canopy of tall trees lies an understorey that receives less sunlight. As a result, plants in the understorey tend to be smaller but with larger leaves to catch sunlight.

GROWING FROM A SEED

When the conditions are right, a plant seed may start to grow. At first, it uses its food store within the seed, but as it grows leaves, which open to catch sunlight, it can start making food through photosynthesis. Its roots draw in water and nutrients from the soil.

1. The seed coating splits and a root starts to grow downwards.

2. The root develops rootlets that branch off and grow into the soil.

3. A stem emerges and begins to grow upwards.

4. The plant grows its first large leaves, supported on its stem.

ASEXUAL REPRODUCTION

Some bacteria reproduce 'asexually' by simply splitting themselves in two. This process is known as binary fission. Each offspring is an exact genetic copy of its parent.

Single bacterium

Cell grows and starts to divide into two

Two daughter cells created

Backbone must support extra weight of foal and fluid carried by the female zebra.

Foal will be able to stand and suckle milk from its mother shortly after it is born.

Foal receives nourishment from the placenta – an organ connected to the side of the uterus.

Bag containing amniotic fluid cushions the foal inside mother when she moves.

EMBRYO GROWTH

Nurtured and kept warm inside a fluid-filled sac, and protected by the wall of the uterus, the tiny human embryo (as it is known at first) rapidly grows. It soon becomes a recognizably human foetus and reaches full size after about 40 weeks.

1. Embryo after six weeks

2. Embryo after eight weeks, now known as a foetus

3. Umbilical cord supplies nutrients to the foetus.

A pregnant zebra carries her developing foal in her uterus, or womb, for a year before she gives birth. This foal's development is almost complete and it will soon be pushed out of its mother's body and be born.

HOW DO CREATURES REPRODUCE?

Reproduction is the creation of offspring – a creature born from existing creatures. In some animals, reproduction takes place with just one parent (asexual), but in others, including humans, it takes place with two parents (sexual).

Asexual reproduction occurs in a number of ways, including budding, found in corals and hydra, where an offspring grows out of the body of the parent. The offspring will be identical to its parent. Sexual reproduction involves specialized sex cells from two parents, most commonly an egg from the female that is fertilized by male sex cells. The offspring will share characteristics of both of its parents but will not be identical to either. Fertilization and development may occur outside the body of the parents or, as in most mammals, the mother may carry the developing young inside her until they are ready to be born live.

Female zebra, called a mare, may be just three years old when she has her first foal.

LAYING EGGS

Insects, birds, amphibians, most fish and monotremes – egg-laying mammals such as the echidna and duck-billed platypus – all lay eggs. Inside an egg, a young creature develops. It is nourished and protected until it hatches.

Female fish may lay thousands of eggs at a time.

HOW DO BEAVERS BUILD A LODGE?

Beavers are plant-eating mammals with extraordinary abilities as home builders. They erect dams across streams to create a pond of still water in which they store food and build their homes, called lodges.

Beavers have poor eyesight, but sharp senses of hearing, smell and touch. They are most comfortable in water and use their remarkably strong teeth to chop and gnaw wood for food and for building materials. Both their dams and lodges are made of branches and sticks carefully piled together and sealed with mud applied by the beaver's large, flat tail. Their tail is also used as a rudder when swimming, to prop the beaver upright when gnawing wood and to signal an alarm over long distances by slapping it hard on the water's surface.

Some sticks pushed into stream bed

1. The beaver begins the dam by laying sticks, branches and rocks on the stream bed. Logs and larger branches are floated into place.

2. Twigs, stones and other materials are laid in front of and around the first rows of sticks to build up the dam's height.

Beaver applies and pats down mud using tail.

Dam breaks water's surface, holding the stream back.

3. Mud and clay are pushed up to the dam. This helps stick everything together. When the mixture dries, it makes the dam watertight.

BUILDING A DAM

Beavers work quickly and at night, carrying mud and stones with their forepaws and timber between their teeth.

A family of beavers gathers branches close to their lodge. Beavers mostly eat bark, buds and wood from trees such as the poplar, birch or willow. In summer, they add water plants, berries and fruit to their diet.

A beaver's dense fur is made water resistant by a thick oil secreted from near its tail.

INSIDE THE LODGE

A lodge provides beavers with a safe winter retreat with entrances out of sight of most predators. A pair of beavers can build a lodge in just a week. Some lodges are repaired and added to by beaver families and may last 30 years or more.

Entrance to the lodge is hidden underwater and close to the pond bed.

Lodge made of rocks, sticks and branches is sealed with an outer covering of mud.

Beavers live in a small room above the water's surface.

Beavers can gnaw and chew through tree trunks up to 25cm in diameter.

Beavers' large, chisel-edged front teeth grow throughout their lives.

A beaver's lodge is built as an island of sticks and mud in the middle of a still pond of water.

An adult beaver can grow to 1.3m long (including its tail) and weigh up to 27kg.

HOW DO CREATURES WORK TOGETHER?

Many creatures of the same species live in large social groups, herds or colonies. They build homes, care for the young and seek out food together. Sometimes, different species of living things work together so that both benefit in a variety of ways.

Many creatures find that living together in large numbers offers them the greatest chance of survival. Occasionally, two different species offer each other protection in different ways. Clownfish, for example, are covered in a special slimy mucus that allows them to live within the stinging tentacles of sea anemones. These protect the clownfish from predators. In return, clownfish chase away creatures that might feed on sea anemones. Some species offer food to another species in return for a service, such as cleaning or flossing, or, in the case of many plants, dispersing their seeds so that new plants can grow away from the parent plant.

MEERKAT MOB

Meerkats live underground in large social groups called mobs. They come to the surface to forage for insects, small lizards and other food to eat while members of the group act as sentries on the lookout for danger.

Meerkat adult and infant dig down to uncover a scorpion.

Sentries keep watch for predators coming from different directions.

Antbirds perch on a branch above, waiting to catch any insects fleeing the army ants...............

A vast column of army ants marches across a rainforest floor in South America. The ants work together to outnumber and overwhelm their prey, which may include cockroaches, scorpions, crickets and small lizards. Using their stings and strong jaws, an army ant swarm may make thousands of kills every day.

Robber flies hover, hoping to pick off insects escaping the ants.

Ants release a chemical trail for other members of the colony to follow.

HELPING EACH OTHER

When species help each other, both may benefit from the relationship, such as when a bee feeds on nectar from a flower and, in return, disperses the flower's pollen. This rhino has its body cleaned of ticks by oxpecker birds which, in return, get an easy meal.

.... Oxpeckers may signal alarm if a predator approaches, warning the rhino.

TAKE-OFF

Most bats cannot take off from the ground because their wings do not provide enough lift, nor can they run forwards fast enough to take off. Instead, they use the height of their roost to launch themselves into the air.

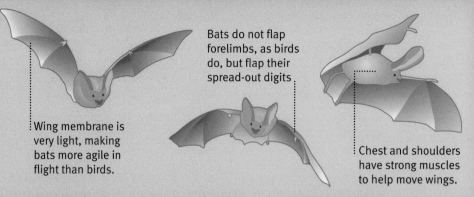

Wing membrane is very light, making bats more agile in flight than birds.

Bats do not flap forelimbs, as birds do, but flap their spread-out digits

Chest and shoulders have strong muscles to help move wings.

Wings fold around the bat's body to keep it warm when resting.

HOW DO BATS SLEEP?

Most bats are nocturnal, meaning that they are active at night and rest during the day. Bats are unusual because they sleep upside down, hanging from a tree branch, cave roof or even the undersides of bridges and tunnels.

Bats sleep in this way for several reasons. It enables them to rest in places that are difficult for daytime predators to spot or reach. It also gives them some height above ground, which helps when they wish to take off (see above). To hang and rest, a bat flies into position, opens the claws on its toes and grips the surface. By letting its body's muscles relax, the weight of the bat hanging down causes its claws to close, locking it into position to rest.

Bats can regrow any small rips in the delicate membrane of their wings.

Thumb claw on wing helps bat to grasp objects.

Bat's head is covered in fur.

A group of bats roosts on branches during the day. These bats are flying foxes, which feed mostly on a diet of fruits and berries. Other bats hunt insects, spiders and even scorpions and small lizards.

Fourth finger forms a supporting rod across the bat's wing membrane.

The bat's wings are spread as it lands on a branch after flight.

Bat sends out short high-pitched pulses of sound that travel outwards and may bounce back off an object as echoes.

Signals bounce back and the bat's brain interprets them to judge direction and distances to objects.

DETECTING PREY

Bats are not blind, yet they often hunt in the dark where their eyesight works poorly. They use echolocation to build a sound map of the area around them and to find and track their prey.

HOW DO CREATURES BREATHE UNDERWATER?

Thousands of different species live in water but still require oxygen for their bodies to respire and produce energy. These creatures obtain oxygen either by surfacing to breathe in air or by extracting oxygen from the water around them.

There are more than 32,000 species of fish, almost all of which do not possess lungs. Instead, they channel water over organs called gills, which draw in oxygen from the water. Other creatures, besides fish, have gills. These include molluscs such as mussels, octopuses and clams. Crabs and other crustaceans, such as shrimp, also possess gills, but some underwater life – bacteria, for example – can absorb oxygen from water through their outer membranes. Marine mammals such as seals, dolphins and whales all possess lungs like land animals do and need to surface regularly to breathe. Some whales can stay underwater for an hour or longer between breaths.

Large gill slits on the underside of the manta ray.

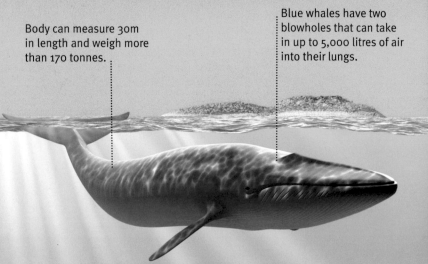

Body can measure 30m in length and weigh more than 170 tonnes.

Blue whales have two blowholes that can take in up to 5,000 litres of air into their lungs.

An average adult manta ray is about 6.5m wide and can weigh 1,300kg.

COMING UP FOR AIR

Cetaceans are a family of mammals that includes whales, dolphins and porpoises. They have nostrils, or blowholes, on top of their heads, which close up when they dive, but open when the creatures surface to breathe in air.

Manta rays are large fish with wing-like pectoral fins that glide gracefully through the water. They feed on about 20–30kg of plankton and fish larvae each day. Like all fish, they obtain oxygen from the sea water using their gills.

GILLS

A fish draws water across its gills. Oxygen diffuses out of the water and into the gill's blood vessels. At the same time, carbon dioxide leaves the blood vessels and exits from the gills.

1. Water is drawn through the fish's mouth, and comb-like gill rakers filter out any food particles from the water.

Gills...............

Gill rakers trap particles...............

Gill filaments

2. As the water moves across the gills, some of the oxygen it contains dissolves in the tiny blood vessels found in the gill filaments.

Oxygen-rich blood flows away from gills.........

Flow of water.

3. Carbon dioxide leaves the blood and enters water. The operculum, a bony flap that covers the gills, opens to let the water flow out of the fish.

Oxygen-poor blood flows to gills..............................

Pectoral fins can flap like wings, helping the fish move through water.

...........Short, narrow tail contains no bones or stinging cells.

FLEXIBLE BONES

Cheetahs have very flexible backbones that bend like a spring with every stride taken, adding power to each step the creature takes.

Long tail helps to balance the cheetah when it runs and turns at high speed.

Long, thin leg bones to which powerful muscles are attached.............

.............Large rib cage to house enlarged heart and lungs.

Dorsal fin grows to 1m high, then retracts when the fish swims at maximum speed, to cut down drag.

Slender, streamlined body helps cut through water fast.............

ACCELERATION

A cheetah can accelerate from a standstill to more than 60km/h in just three strides by using its powerful muscles and flexible skeleton. It can reach 100km/h in only three seconds.

1. Cheetah strides forwards, pushing off its hard footpads and dropping its head slightly.

2. Spine bends and coils up like a spring as the rear legs travel forwards.

3. Spine uncoils at the same time as leg muscles push the cheetah forwards with great power, taking a 7.5m-long bound.

.............Strong tail can swing back and forth to generate the great power needed to swim quickly.

Upper jaw forms long, sword-like bill, at least twice the length of lower jaw.

A sailfish leaps out of the water. This large ocean fish can swim at speeds of 60–65km/h for long periods of time. When chasing prey or evading capture, its powerful body and tail can propel it to speeds of 110km/h.

HOW DO THE FASTEST CREATURES ACCELERATE?

The fastest creatures on land, as well as in the air and sea, use their great speed to catch other fast-moving prey. They are all streamlined so that they can move through air or water with as little resistance as possible.

Each record-breaking creature has adaptations to their body that help them move as rapidly and as efficiently as possible. The cheetah, for example, is lightweight – usually weighing less than 60kg – and has a larger heart and lungs than other mammals of a similar size. These help to supply its body with enough oxygen during its high-speed sprints of up to 120km/h. Both the sailfish (the fastest fish) and the peregrine falcon (the fastest bird) can pull in body parts to create as smooth, sleek and fast a shape as possible, and have powerful muscles to drive them forwards.

Pointed mouth catches fish and crustaceans.

Sailfish can grow to 2.5–3.1m long and weigh 90kg.

FASTEST FLIER

Peregrine falcons fly to high altitudes and dive steeply in order to catch their prey. As they dive, their pointed wings are tucked in tightly to create a shape that cuts through the air easily. These birds can reach speeds of up to 320km/h.

Slim, stiff feathers

Pointed wings tucked in during dive for high speed.

HOW DO ANIMALS MIGRATE?

Many living things go on long migration journeys at the same time each year. They go in search of food, water, a place to breed and reproduce, or, as the seasons change, an environment with a more suitable climate.

Often, migrating animals travel in large numbers – in herds, flocks or schools that offer them protection and help in finding the way. Some species may use familiar geographical landmarks and certain smells and tastes as a guide. Others may be able to sense changes in Earth's magnetic field, giving them an internal compass that helps them to find north or south. Animals also have to know when to migrate, and often use changes in temperature or 'photoperiod' – the amount of daylight in a day – as a guide. Shorter days tell them that winter is approaching.

Every year, a great herd of wildebeest travels up to 2,500km across Africa's Serengeti Plain. The animals go in search of the lush, mineral-rich grasslands that help to keep them healthy. Herds can include hundreds of thousands of individuals.

Wildebeest follow the herd up a steep bank on their way to food-rich grasslands.

Each front hoof of a wildebeest leaves a trail of scent for other wildebeest to follow.

MONARCH BUTTERLY

These butterflies cannot survive the winters of Canada and the northern United States. At the end of every summer they fly south, travelling up to 4,400km to spend the winter in Mexico or California.

Antenna helps the butterfly to navigate, using the Sun as a guide.

Wingspan measures 10cm at its widest point.

Butterfly's abdomen contains its heart and most of its digestive system.

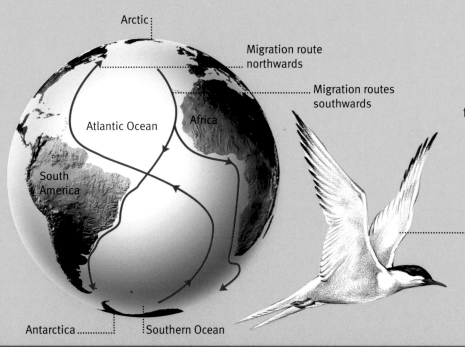

Arctic

Migration route
northwards

Migration routes
southwards

Atlantic Ocean

Africa

South
America

Antarctica

Southern Ocean

ARCTIC TERN

Every August or September,
Arctic terns make an
astonishing, long-range
migration from deep inside
the Arctic Circle to Antarctica,
flying down the African or
South American coastline.
They return to the Arctic
the following spring.

Arctic tern's wingspan
is 76–85cm, yet the
bird is light, weighing
as little as 100g.

CARIBOU HERDS

Each year, herds of caribou migrate to the
open Arctic tundra in summer, where they
eat up to 5kg of plants a day. In winter, herds
move to forest regions, sometimes swimming
across lakes and sea bays along the way.

Clouds of dust billow up from
the trampling of the ground by
all the wildebeests' hooves.

81

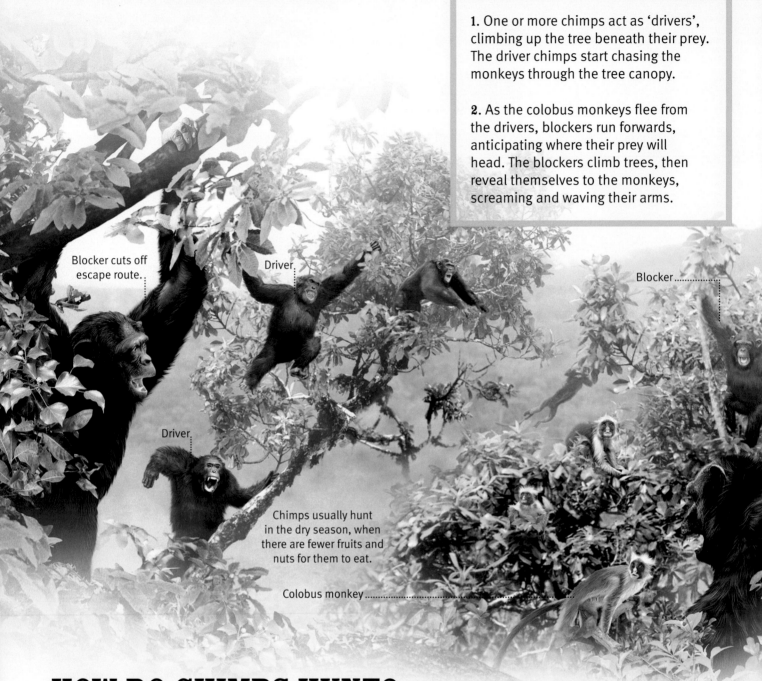

1. One or more chimps act as 'drivers', climbing up the tree beneath their prey. The driver chimps start chasing the monkeys through the tree canopy.

2. As the colobus monkeys flee from the drivers, blockers run forwards, anticipating where their prey will head. The blockers climb trees, then reveal themselves to the monkeys, screaming and waving their arms.

Blocker cuts off escape route.

Driver

Blocker

Driver

Chimps usually hunt in the dry season, when there are fewer fruits and nuts for them to eat.

Colobus monkey

HOW DO CHIMPS HUNT?

Chimpanzees in West Africa eat fruit, nuts and leaves, but sometimes go hunting. Red colobus monkeys, which are light, agile and good at leaping from tree to tree, are the chimpanzees' main prey. Chimps are heavy, with some weighing nearly as much as a man. On its own, a chimp could not catch a colobus. But by working together in cunning ways, chimps can herd colobus monkeys into a trap.

3. The terrified monkeys are driven between the blockers. Ahead hides an ambusher – the most experienced hunter in the group of chimps – who lies in wait for the fleeing monkeys.

4. The ambusher attacks. If a colobus spots the ambusher and tries to retreat, it will probably fall prey to one of the other chimps in the hunting party.

HOW DO CARNIVOROUS PLANTS TRAP PREY?

Carnivorous (meat-eating) plants trap and digest flies, insects and spiders. The Venus fly trap grows in bogs where the acidic soil lacks certain nutrients the plant needs. So it lures insects to its leaves by producing sweet, sticky nectar, then digests them to make up for the missing nutrients.

This Venus fly trap is one of more than 500 types of carnivorous plant.

Long cilia lock together to trap prey.

Ambusher shows himself at the last minute.

1. Each pair of leaves has three 'trigger' hairs. If an insect walks over two triggers in a 20- to 30-second period, the fly trap springs into action.

2. The leaves snap shut in half a second. Finger-like prongs called cilia, around the edge of each leaf, keep larger insects inside. Smaller insects, not worth digesting, are able to escape.

3. The leaves close fully, trapping the insect. The plant pumps out digestive juices that dissolve the soft, inner parts of the insect but leave any hard, bony parts.

4. Digestion takes 5–12 days. Then the leaves open, the leftover body parts are blown away or washed away by rain, and the plant is ready for its next victim.

SUPER-FAST SNAP
Bladderworts are underwater carnivorous plants. Some species have the fastest traps of all, taking just 1/30th of a second to capture prey – many times faster than a Venus fly trap.

HOW DO SHARKS SENSE PREY?

Sharks are among the natural world's most accomplished predators, able to detect and hunt down prey from long distances away. Key to their success is the large range of sophisticated and accurate senses they possess.

Sharks have large eyes that give them keen eyesight in gloomy, deep water where there's little light. A shark uses its hearing to pick up low-frequency sounds. It also has an exceptionally strong sense of smell (see right), and can even detect tiny electrical signals given off by other sea creatures' hearts and muscles. This enables sharks to seek out prey that may be hiding in sand on the ocean floor. Once the prey is located, sharks move quickly and attack with powerful jaws filled with large, sharp teeth.

Large stomach secretes powerful acids to digest any prey caught and eaten.

Powerful tail muscles and fin help propel the shark through water at speeds up to 24km/h.

Pectoral fins are used to lift and steer the body as it travels forward.

Torpedo-shaped body is streamlined to travel quickly and easily through water.

SENSE RANGES

A shark's senses work at different distances. For example, sharks sense water temperature and touch only through their skin, but they can detect sounds over many kilometres.

Vision up to 50m

Smell (used from 100m up to several kilometres)

Electrical signals up to 50cm

Vibrations sensed as changes in water pressure (up to 100m)

Hearing (used over distances of more than 1km)

| 0 | 1m | 10m | 100m | 1,000m | 10,000 m |

A great white shark swoops to catch a seal in its giant, teeth-lined jaws. These fearsome predatory fish, one of more than 400 species of shark, can grow to between 4.6m and 6.4m long and weigh as much as 3,000kg.

Shark's snout is flexible and cushioned for impact with the body of its prey.

SHARK'S HEAD

As fish, sharks have gills that obtain oxygen from water. They have nostrils, but use them for smell and not for breathing. Some sharks can smell a small amount of blood in the water from more than 1,500m away.

Nostrils channel water into nasal cavities where sense organs detect smells.

Forward-facing eyes can judge distances to objects accurately.

Lower jaw is hinged and opens widely to catch large prey.

Mouth filled with as many as 300 triangular-shaped teeth in rows.

Lateral line

LATERAL LINE

A long row of tiny, fluid-filled vessels called neuromasts run the length of a shark's body. These help it to sense vibrations in water caused by the movement of injured fish or marine mammals thrashing around.

85

A diamondback rattlesnake, so named for its distinctive body markings, closes in on a collared lizard, ready for the kill. The snake will strike with its large, curved fangs and inject venom into the lizard. This type of snake also preys upon small mammals.

Rattle on the end of its tail may warn predators or hoofed animals away from the snake.

Long, flexible body may grow up to 2–2.5m in length.

HOW DO SNAKES KILL?

Snakes are carnivores equipped with a large range of senses used for hunting, and often ambushing, their prey. While their eyesight is not well developed, their senses of hearing, touch, and especially taste and smell, are strong.

Snakes flick their tongue to collect airborne particles that they wipe on the roof of their mouth. There, a special organ known as the Jacobson's organ helps the brain to identify smells. Rattlesnakes have highly sensitive heat-sensing organs between their eyes and nose that can track prey in total darkness. Many snakes are venomous, using fangs to inject poison into their prey. Others capture and swallow prey whole, or may first wrap their body tightly around it and squeeze it to death. Some snakes have unusual killing methods. The Australian Woma python, for example, pushes and crushes small rodents against the wall of its prey's burrow.

SWALLOWING WHOLE

A snake cannot chew its prey, so it must swallow it whole. Very flexible jaws allow it to swallow prey much larger than itself. The snake becomes dormant while it digests, but may regurgitate (bring up) the prey if it needs to escape danger.

VENOMOUS SNAKES

A snake's venom is produced and stored in a pair of venom glands, one under each eye. Venom varies in strength between different snakes, but it contains toxins that damage the prey's heart and blood vessels, and may cause its breathing to stop.

Venom gland

Fangs unfold to point downwards.

Venom travels down venom canal.

Prey is poisoned and eaten.

1. Snake opens its mouth to strike. The snake's venom travels down a tube and into the fangs.

2. The snake closes its mouth, sinking its fangs into the body of its prey and injecting venom.

3. Venom enters the prey's bloodstream. It may kill within minutes or paralyse the victim so that the snake can swallow it whole.

Rattlesnake's nostrils can detect smells over long distances.

Lower jaw is divided into two parts and is jointed so that the snake can open its mouth very wide.

CONSTRICTORS

Constrictors, such as boas, pythons and anacondas, strike by wrapping their muscular bodies in coils around the body of their prey. As they apply great pressure, their victims' breathing and heart stop. The prey is then swallowed whole and may take weeks to digest.

Flicking tongue catches scent particles in the air and helps the snake to identify smells.

Every part of this lizard, apart from its nails or claws, will be dissolved and absorbed in the snake's powerful digestive system.

HOW DO SPECIES BECOME ENDANGERED?

All around the world, hundreds of different living things – from plants and insects to birds, fish and large mammals – are endangered. This means that an entire species may become extinct (die out). There are many reasons why this can occur.

Throughout Earth's natural history, species of living things have flourished and then become extinct. In recent centuries, however, the increasing impact of human activity on the environment has meant that many successful species are faced with the threat of extinction. Pollution from industrial processes and accidents such as chemical and oil spills have damaged environments and threatened certain species. Other threatening activities include overfishing and hunting animals for food and fur, or, in the case of rhinos, for their horns. One of the most common threats in some parts of the world is habitat destruction. This is where the natural homes and environments of living things are destroyed, by draining wetlands or cutting down forests, for example.

Here, a polar bear hunts a beluga whale. Polar bears in some areas of the Arctic are endangered because of pollution and climate change, which is melting the Arctic sea ice where many polar bears live.

Rear legs are used in water as a rudder for steering.

In the water, polar bears normally swim using their front legs.

Polar bears are able to dive to depths of up to 4.5m and stay underwater for more than a minute.

JAGUAR

Today, the Americas' largest big cat, the jaguar, is endangered because people hunt it for its beautiful fur coat, and because the forest habitats where the jaguars live are being destroyed.

Powerful jaws used to kill prey with one crushing bite.

Front paws contain retractable claws that spring out when hunting.

Fur covers a thick layer of blubber that insulates the polar bear and keeps it warm.

Large parts of the Borneo rainforest are undisturbed and unexplored.

Borneo Island

1950

Trees are cleared as farming, industry and human settlements spread.

Borneo Island

2010

SHRINKING FORESTS

The scale of habitat destruction becomes clear when we look at how dramatically the world's forests have shrunk over the past 10,000 years as the human population has grown. The Borneo rainforest (above) has shrunk rapidly in just 60 years, as trees have been cleared for farmland or new settlements, or for timber or firewood.

Short, curved claws can dig into and grip prey.

CANE TOADS

Species introduced by humans to new regions can sometimes spread and destroy populations of other living things. A handful of cane toads were introduced into Australia in the 1930s. They now number many millions, compete for food with other species and kill frogs, quolls and other creatures with their poisonous skin.

Jaws and teeth are used to bite and kill seals, walruses and small whales.

HOW DO OXYGEN AND NUTRIENTS TRAVEL?

Humans need oxygen to be constantly carried around their bodies. Cells use this oxygen to release energy from sugars during the process of respiration. They also need nutrients to be transported through their bodies. Both tasks are performed by the blood in the circulatory system.

The human body contains about five litres of blood, which is constantly circulated throughout the body by the heart – a large, muscular pump with four chambers. This pumps (beats) about 70 times every minute, effectively moving approximately 7,500 litres of blood around the body every day. The blood travels inside a vast network of blood vessels to all parts of the body, delivering oxygen to cells and carrying away waste carbon dioxide. Nutrients from digested food are mostly absorbed into blood from the small intestine so that they can then be carried throughout the body as well.

Here, a blood vessel is cut away to reveal the blood cells travelling through it. More than half of blood is made up of plasma – a thin, watery substance that carries absorbed nutrients and vitamins around the body.

Right atrium

Oxygen-rich blood leaves the heart via the aorta – the largest blood vessel in the body.

Pulmonary artery carries blood from heart to lungs.

Pulmonary veins carry blood from lungs back to the heart.

Left atrium

Right ventricle

Left ventricle

BEATING HEART

Blood low in oxygen enters the first heart chamber, the right atrium. From there, it is pumped through the right ventricle up and out of the heart to the lungs, where it obtains more oxygen. The blood returns to the left atrium and travels to the left ventricle, from where it is pumped out and around the body.

White blood cell helps fight infections and germs.

Oxygen binds with a substance called haemoglobin in red blood cells. This gives blood its colour.

90

Wall of blood vessel is thin.

CIRCULATORY SYSTEM

Over 95,000km of blood vessels make up the circulatory system's transport network, carrying blood to and from the heart. Arteries carry blood away from the heart, while veins carry blood towards the heart.

Jugular vein carries oxygen-poor blood from the brain towards the heart.

In the lungs, oxygen is added to blood and carbon dioxide removed.

Femoral artery carries blood into the upper leg.

Platelets clot (stick together) in the presence of air to help seal a damaged blood vessel.

Doughnut-shaped red blood cell

HOW DO HUMANS RUN?

Running fast requires a number of the human body's major systems to work well together. These include the muscular system as well as the skeleton and its joints, which provide the moving framework that supports the rest of the body.

More than 600 skeletal muscles are attached to bones via tendons. These muscles contract (get shorter) or relax to provide the force that moves the body's parts. Running involves far more muscles than just those that lift and drive the legs forwards to take long, quick strides. The arms must pump back and forth while the muscles in the core of the body must be strong to maintain a balanced posture. Working your muscles hard to run at high speed makes great demands on other parts of your body. The rate of breathing increases to draw in more oxygen and the heart beats faster to pump blood around the body more quickly, so that oxygen and nutrients can reach the muscles.

An athlete starts a race, pushing his legs out of the starting blocks in order to sprint down a track. Many muscles in his body must work together efficiently for him to run smoothly and quickly.

Gluteus maximus muscle is the largest individual muscle in the human body. It helps maintain the body's posture. ....

Hamstring muscle bends leg at the knee. ....

MUSCLE CONTRACTION

Each skeletal muscle is made of large bundles of long cells called fibres. Nerve signals travel from the brain to the muscles, causing the muscle fibres to contract and pull the bones to which they are attached.

Muscle fibre relaxes

Muscle fibre contracts

Rear foot drives hard ....
out of the starting
block as the leg
straightens.

Gastrocnemius muscle bends foot downwards and also flexes the knee.

Deltoid muscle helps move arm backwards and then forwards during run.

Head kept down in first few paces of sprint but will lift as the body rises.

Biceps relaxes as triceps contracts to pull arm downwards.

Biceps contracts to pull lower arm up.

Triceps relaxes

ANTAGONISTIC PAIRS

A single muscle can pull parts of the body only in one direction. So muscles are grouped around the body in antagonistic pairs, such as the biceps and triceps muscles in your upper arm. Together, they can move the arm in different directions.

Biceps muscle helps bend arm at the elbow.

Front leg drives up and forward to take the first stride in the run.

THE FASTEST MAN ALIVE

Usain Bolt of Jamaica crosses the finishing line to win a men's sprint race. In 2009, Bolt ran the world's fastest ever 100m time of 9.58 seconds, averaging a speed throughout the race of 37.58km/h.

Runner will land on the ball of his foot.

HOW DO OPTICAL ILLUSIONS FOOL THE BRAIN?

Optical illusions use colour, light and patterns to create images that trick your brain into seeing something that is not there, or mislead it in some other way. This happens for a range of reasons.

For a strong sense of vision, your brain must process millions of signals from your eyes continuously. It must make sense of the signals using experience and knowledge, looking for patterns and recognizable objects. Sometimes it fills in gaps to see objects it is familiar with, or groups random objects together in patterns it understands. Optical illusions make use of the way the brain makes assumptions. They trick it into filling in a shape or misjudging the sizes of two same-sized objects.

Occipital lobe at rear of brain is the main vision centre, processing signals sent from the eyes.

Brain stem links spinal cord and brain.

Nerves branch out from the spinal cord to reach all over the body.

Spinal cord carries large numbers of signals from all parts of the body to the brain.

NERVOUS SYSTEM

A vast network of nerve fibres, each made up of neurons (nerve cells), runs through the human body carrying signals. Sensory nerves carry signals to the brain from parts of the body, while motor nerves carry instructions from the brain to move muscles, for example.

WHICH IS LONGER?

The bottom horizontal line appears shorter, but it is an optical illusion. Both lines are the same length. Your brain is tricked by the different angle of the arrowheads to believe that the top horizontal line is longer.

Skull, made up of bony plates, protects the delicate brain inside. ....

To read words on the page or view pictures, the eye must focus on the page and send signals captured by its retina (see below) along the optic nerve to the brain.

Lacrimal gland secretes tears .... that keep the front of the eye moist and wash away dust and dirt.

The eye's curved lens is protected by a transparent cover called the cornea. ....

Image signals collected by retina at back of eye. ....

Pupil adjusts amount of light let into the eye. ....

The eye is held in its skull socket by a series of muscles called the muscles of orbit. They control the movement of the eye.

Lens focuses image, which travels through the pupil into the eye. ....

INSIDE THE EYE

Light passes through the clear lens of the eye, which focuses it on the rear of the eye – the retina. There, light-sensitive rod and cone cells convert the image into electrical signals sent to the brain via the optic nerve.

LIFE
FIND OUT MORE ABOUT HOW THE WORLD WORKS

WEBSITES TO VISIT

www.nhm.ac.uk/nature-online/life/mammals/migration/index.html
Learn more about animal migrations from the website of the Natural History Museum, London, UK.

www.mnh.si.edu/ants/photogallery/index.htm
A fascinating gallery of photos from the Smithsonian Museum of Natural History, Washington D.C., USA, shows how ants live and work in colonies.

www.bats.org.uk
Find out lots more about bats and how they live at the web pages of the Bat Conservation Trust.

www.sharktrust.org
Learn the facts about one of the most misunderstood groups of creatures on the planet, sharks. This website includes a database of shark species and facts on shark biology.

www.cheetah.org
The Cheetah Conservation Fund website contains images and facts about the world's fastest land mammal.

http://animal.discovery.com/guides/endangered/endangered.html
Pick up valuable and accurate information on more than 240 different endangered species.

www.bhf.org.uk/heart-health/how-your-heart-works.aspx
See how a healthy heart works at these web pages brought to you by the British Heart Foundation.

http://faculty.washington.edu/chudler/introb.html
Explore the brain and nervous system, and learn about brain development, the nervous system, nerve disorders and much, much more at this website hosted by neuroscientist Dr Eric H Chudler.

http://science.howstuffworks.com/life/human-biology/eye1.htm
Learn more about how the human eye works and enables us to see.

http://kids.niehs.nih.gov/games/illusions/index.htm
Enjoy this large collection of optical illusions at the USA's National Institute of Environmental Health Sciences' web pages for children.

BOOKS TO LOOK OUT FOR

• THE KINGFISHER ANIMAL ENCYCLOPEDIA by David Burnie (Kingfisher, 2011)

• HUMAN BODY FACTORY by Dan Green (Kingfisher, 2012)

• THE KINGFISHER ENCYCLOPEDIA OF LIFE (Kingfisher, 2012)

• REALLY REALLY BIG QUESTIONS ABOUT ME by Dr Stephen Law (Kingfisher, 2012)

• WHO AM I? by Richard Walker (Kingfisher, 2012)

CHAPTER FOUR
SCIENCE AND TECHNOLOGY

HOW ARE COMPUTER GAMES CREATED?

Console computer games are the work of large teams. A game starts out as a story idea that is then storyboarded (sketched out) by games designers to portray all the different scenes and options that can occur.

The storyboard gives a visual plot of the game and how it can be played. It must allow for every outcome that a player may choose during the game. A large team of artists and animators design all the game's scenes, objects and characters. Others work on the music and sound effects, while voice actors record the game dialogue. As all the different parts come together, the game is tested rigorously for any bugs (flaws or errors). Sometimes, an early version of the game is released to experienced gamers so they can test it fully and identify any problems.

Key details of the character's clothing or equipment are built up over the exoskeleton.

A pirate character for a computer game goes through a number of development stages after it is drawn on paper by artists. The final model is a lifelike 3D figure that can be programmed to move all of its parts in the computer game.

A series of 3D shapes, known as a polygon mesh, make up the basic shape of the character.

A grid of lines forms the character's frame, called an exoskeleton, and is animated by computer.

Character's skin and clothing are rendered (finished in detail) by computers to give a realistic 3D appearance.

GAME PROGRAMMING

Behind the scenes and action in a game lie thousands, sometimes millions, of lines of computer code that generate the environment, the game's rules and the ways by which characters and objects move. Teams of programmers are responsible for getting all this code correct and fully working.

MOTION CAPTURE

National Basketball Association (NBA) star Tony Parker wears a motion-control suit. Game designers are using data from the suit to capture Parker's movements accurately on a computer for use in a basketball game.

Sensors called trackers record body movements.

HOW DO ROBOTS FIND THEIR WAY?

Mobile robots can move from place to place on land, in the air, in space or under water. Many are remote-controlled from a distance by a human operator, but some robots navigate themselves to their target.

A robot has a range of devices called sensors. These gather information about the robot itself and the area around it and send the data to the robot's controller, usually an onboard computer. The controller makes decisions based on the data and instructs all the parts of the robot. Some mobile robots are equipped with many different sensors that build up a detailed data picture of their environment. This information may be used with a global positioning system (GPS) to plot the robot's route, while proximity sensors measure the distances to obstacles and objects.

Two different mobile robots attend to an injured soldier. The larger is a Battlefield Extraction-Assist Robot (BEAR). In the future, robots like these may work by themselves, finding wounded soldiers or injured people to lift and rescue in disaster areas.

Sensors inside track units tell the robot's controller the speed and angle at which they're moving.

Tracks allow the robot to climb over obstacles and travel across rough ground.

Laser rangefinder sensor helps the robot's controller judge the distances to objects ahead.

UNDERWATER ROBOTS
Some robots can navigate underwater for voyages lasting many days or weeks at a time. Many use sonar, which bounces high-pitch sound signals off nearby objects to determine the objects' distance from the robot.

Hydraulic-powered arms can lift more than 200kg. They slide under the figure on the ground and lift him up.

Cameras in the robot's head process views of the terrain.

Bulging nose houses a large dish that sends and receives signals from the ground.

GLOBAL HAWK

This unmanned aerial vehicle (UAV) can travel long distances to spy on the land below. In 2001, a Global Hawk became the first unmanned aircraft to cross the Pacific Ocean. Its non-stop flight took more than 22 hours.

Single jet engine can keep Global Hawk airborne for up to 36 hours.

In the future, soldiers may carry a tracking sensor that will allow a robot to locate their position and come to their aid.

Single red blood cell is almost as big as the entire nanobot

Legs propel the nanobot forwards, 'swimming' through the bloodstream.

A future medical nanobot, smaller than a grain of sand, travels through a person's bloodstream. It is one of thousands entering the body via a single injection. It will seek out and tackle diseases from the inside.

Robot's body is made of carbon nanotubes and other nano-engineered materials.

HOW WILL NANOTECHNOLOGY CHANGE THE WORLD?

Nanotechnology devices are measured in nanometres – one nanometre is equal to one-billionth of a metre. To give an idea of this scale, a single hair is about 80,000 nanometres thick. Nanotechnology could transform many areas of technology.

If technology is shrunk down to the nano level, it may work faster and require far less energy to power it. It may be possible to create clothing that can change its colour or texture at a single command, or shrink computer memory so that data is stored as individual atoms – which would greatly speed up computer power. In the future, small nano-factories, not much larger than a kitchen breadmaker, may be capable of mass-producing thousands of robots, measuring mere nanometres in size. These nanobots might then be used to tackle pollution, fight disease inside the body and repair other machines.

MICRO GEARS

Scientists have already had great success with MEMS (microelectromechanical systems) – machinery built larger than nanotechnology but still to tiny fractions of a millimetre. This set of microscopic gears is 1/100th the thickness of a piece of paper.

Nanotechnology may help to create truly flexible screens, allowing future computer or mobile phone users to roll up a large-sized computer screen and put it in their pocket.

Chemical sensors seek out diseased cells for the robot to tackle.

Gripper arms can fasten onto diseased cell and inject tiny quantities of drugs.

NANOTUBES

Individual carbon atoms can be rolled into long and incredibly slender cylinders that are only a few nanometres in diameter. These 'nanotube' structures are extremely light and strong, and can conduct electricity.

Carbon atoms form a hexagon (six-sided) pattern in a nanotube.

FUEL RODS

The reactor's energy is generated inside its nuclear fuel rods. These are sealed metal rods containing pellets made of uranium oxide, a radioactive substance. Reactions from the nuclear fission (see box opposite) create the energy that heats the water.

.... Control rod

.... Concrete shield

.... Fuel rod

.... Graphite core

1. Inside the solid steel reactor, fuel rods made of uranium are arranged in bundles.

2. Control rods are lowered into the core to slow down nuclear reactions. The control rods are made of materials that absorb the neutrons emitted by the fuel rods.

Cooling towers condense the steam from the turbine, turning it back into liquid water.

Sealed, pressurized reactor tank made of thick steel.

Reactor encased in a thick, protective concrete layer.

Water pumped into bottom of reactor is heated to turn into steam.

Nuclear reactor containment building

Steam under high pressure is piped to the turbines

Turned by a shaft from the turbine, the generator produces electricity.

Steam turbine consists of many blades turned round by the high-pressure steam.

Turbine hall houses the generators and steam turbines.

SPLITTING ATOMS

When the nucleus of an atom is split, the energy that holds the atom together is released, as well as tiny particles called neutrons. These neutrons can hit other nuclei in other atoms, making them split and causing a chain reaction.

Single neutron fires towards unstable nucleus of a uranium atom.

Nucleus splits into smaller nuclei and free neutrons.

Energy released as a result of reaction.

Free neutrons will strike other nuclei, causing a chain reaction.

HOW DOES NUCLEAR POWER WORK?

About 13 per cent of the world's electricity is generated by nuclear power stations. These use the energy created by splitting the nucleus of atoms (a process called nuclear fission) to drive giant electricity-generating turbines.

A nuclear power station is made up of a large reactor, steam-driven turbines and electricity generators all connected via numerous control and safety systems. Many nuclear power stations are situated on the coast so that seawater can be used in their cooling processes.

Nuclear power stations rely on a chain reaction within their fuel rods to generate huge amounts of energy. This energy heats water into steam that drives turbines. The turbines, in turn, power electricity generators. Electricity is carried to where it is needed by power lines. Nuclear power is reliable and – unlike power stations fuelled by coal or oil – does not emit polluting gases into the atmosphere. But fears remain about accidents that may cause radioactive leaks harmful to living things.

HOW DO WIND FARMS WORK?

A wind farm is a collection of wind turbines that may be grouped together on land or out at sea. Each wind turbine uses the power of the wind to turn its propeller-like rotor blades in order to generate electricity.

A large group of wind turbines form a wind farm in the sea. Automatic controllers inside each turbine monitor the wind speed and weather conditions, and may shut the turbine down if the wind reaches dangerously high speeds.

Wind farms may be small or large collections of wind turbines. The Walney Wind Farm off the northwest coast of England, for example, comprises 102 turbines. The turbines themselves can vary in size – from small models suitable for a single house to giants standing nearly 200m tall and with a rotor diameter of 126m. Large wind turbines can be expensive to build and some people object to their spoiling the landscape or generating a lot of noise. However, wind energy will not run out and can generate electricity cheaply and cleanly without creating harmful emissions that pollute the atmosphere.

Tall tower made out of steel, concrete or a combination of both.

Incoming wind direction

Rotor blades turn, spinning a central shaft that runs through a gearbox.

GENERATORS

Generators make electricity by turning a wire coil through a magnetic field. A wind turbine provides the mechanical turning power for the generator via its rotor blades, which are moved by the wind.

The turning coil inside the generator induces an electric current.

DIFFERENT DESIGNS

Wind turbines come in different shapes and designs. Some have blades that turn on a vertical axis instead of horizontally. These may generate less electricity but they take up less space and can operate closer to the ground, like these colourful Savonius turbines in a city park.

Curved blades catch the wind and spin, turning the turbine to generate electricity.

Anemometer measures wind speed.

The blades and the turbine body, called the nacelle, turn to point into the wind.

Generator inside the turbine generates electricity.

Angle of each rotor blade, called its pitch, can be adjusted depending on the wind's direction.

HOW CAN WE BE MORE ENERGY EFFICIENT?

Energy efficiency is about using less energy overall to perform tasks. In the home, improved energy efficiency can be achieved by using less power-hungry devices, and by reducing heat loss from a building.

Rising energy costs and concern about the potential harm to the planet caused by certain types of energy has seen more homes adopt energy-efficient technology or practices. Fitting more energy-efficient lights and electrical appliances, reducing central heating temperatures and turning off electrical items when not in use all help to reduce energy use, as can insulating roofs and walls to stop heat escaping. Along with energy efficiency, more and more people are using renewable energies such as solar and wind power as well as geothermal power (heat from the Earth). These are forms of energy that do not release harmful emissions into the atmosphere and will not run out.

Roof is covered in grass, which helps insulate house and reduce heat loss.

Solar panels are made up of a series of photovoltaic cells that generate electricity from sunlight.

Windows are triple glazed to stop heat leaking out.

SOLAR POWER

Photovoltaic cells are made up of semiconducting materials, such as silicon, that release electrons when struck by light. These electrons flow as a current that can be used by an electrical circuit to power electrical devices.

Light rays strike panel

Each cell generates a small electric voltage between two semiconductors.

Solar panel contains many photovoltaic cells.

Electric current flows through wiring to light bulb.

This innovative eco-home is a passive house, meaning that it generates its own energy and does not take electricity from the supply grid. It is built into the ground, which helps keep warmth in.

Domestic wind turbine generates enough electricity to light the house.

Thick plastic foam between the outer and inner walls helps keep warmth in the house.

Underfloor heating system uses heat obtained from the geothermal piping.

Geothermal piping full of liquid draws in heat from the soil.

LOW-ENERGY BULB

Compact fluorescent lamps (CFLs) generate light by passing electricity through a tube full of gases. These gases give off ultraviolet light, which causes a phosphor coating on the tube to shine. CFLs last longer and use a fraction of the energy used by traditional bulbs.

Phosphor coating on tube emits light.

Spiralling tube contains argon and mercury gases.

Ballast produces an electric current that flows through the tube.

Fitting for bulb socket

HEAT LOSS

This heat image of a wooden-framed house glows yellow where heat energy loss is at its greatest – through the single-glazed windows and poorly insulated front walls of the home.

CANTILEVER BRIDGE

This type of bridge is built outwards from each vertical tower. To complete the span, a central beam connects each arm.

Forth Rail Bridge, Scotland
(built 1883–90)

The Millau Viaduct is a cable-stayed bridge. It looks similar to a suspension bridge, but the road deck is supported by the masts, not by anchors at each end.

Concrete towers rose at a rate of 4m per day.

Temporary towers were taken down at the end.

Hydraulic jacks pushed the temporary towers up 1m at a time.

HOW IS A SUPERBRIDGE BUILT?

Today, lightweight steel and other extra-strong materials allow engineers to build enormous bridges that span rivers, valleys and seas. The Millau Viaduct in France is a record-breaker – the tallest bridge ever built.

Opened in 2004, the viaduct took ten years to plan and three to build, at a cost of £270 million. First, seven giant, reinforced concrete towers were built up from the valley floor. Next, hydraulic jacks and wedges pushed out steel decks for carrying the road from each side of the valley – 3cm at a time. Temporary steel towers were built between the concrete ones to reduce the distance over which the decking had to be supported. Finally, the temporary towers were taken down.

SUSPENSION BRIDGE

In this type of bridge, the cables are attached to massive anchorages at each end. These support the weight of the road deck.

Golden Gate Bridge, San Francisco, USA
(built 1933–37)

The tallest mast top is 343m above the river – higher than the top of the Eiffel Tower in Paris, France.

ARCH BRIDGE
This is one of the oldest bridge designs. The weight is carried down the arch to massive supports at each end.

Sydney Harbour Bridge, Australia (built 1923–32)

Steel stays (cables), anchored to seven masts, support the road deck.

Road deck is built of steel, not concrete, to make it lighter and slimmer.

MOVING THE ROAD DECK
1. A lifting wedge is pushed out, moving the pushing wedge and deck upwards.

2. A cylinder or jack moves the pushing wedge and deck forwards.

3. The lifting wedge is pulled back. The pushing wedge and deck are dropped.

4. The pushing wedge is moved back to its original position.

Jack pushes out.

Jack pulls in.

Pushing wedge

Lifting wedge

TUNNEL LINING

After tunnels are bored or cut out, their walls have to be reinforced quickly before they collapse, usually with a framework made of steel and a lining made of concrete. The tunnel is then finished with fittings such as a roadway or railway tracks, and with lighting and safety systems.

A machine spreads concrete in the Gotthard Base Tunnel in Switzerland.

Prefabricated, curved concrete walls support the newly bored tunnel.

Conveyor belts powered by electric motors carry rock chips away from the tunnel boring machine.

HOW ARE TUNNELS BUILT?

Tunnels are used to carry large quantities of water from reservoirs to cities. They also provide trains and motor vehicles with quick, convenient routes through hills and mountains, under seas and rivers and beneath cities.

Before boring a tunnel, engineers analyse soil and rock samples and drill test holes to investigate the ground they are about to dig through. Some shallow tunnels are built using a cut and cover method where a 'U'-shaped trench is dug and then a strong roof fitted over it, turning it into a tunnel. Many larger and deeper tunnels are now built using gigantic tunnel boring machines (TBMs). These giant, cylinder-shaped machines are lowered into the first part of a tunnel shaft and then slowly creep forward as their cutting head grates and grinds the rock away.

Hydraulic rams (powerful pistons) push the cutter head into the rock face.

A giant tunnel-boring machine (TBM) works inside the Gotthard Base Tunnel underneath the Swiss Alps. The tunnel is in fact a pair of 57km-long tunnels. They will be the world's longest railway tunnels when completed in 2016–17.

TBMs limit the disturbance to the surrounding ground and produce a smooth tunnel wall.

CUTTING HEAD

A TBM with a cutting head 6m in diameter breaks through the rock after boring a 6.4km-long tunnel through the San Bernardino Mountains. The tunnel is designed to deliver water to parts of California, USA.

Powerful pneumatic jacks can be raised or lowered to alter the direction of tunnelling.

Tunnel workers are dwarfed by giant TBM that cuts the tunnel at a typical rate of 70cm per hour.

Rock chips travel through gaps in the rotating cutting head and are carried back from the TBM for collection by other machines.

Cutting head is fitted with sharp, tough, steel cutting discs that cause fractures in the rock face and chip it away.

HOW DO HIGH-SPEED TRAINS RUN?

The first high-speed train service in the world was the Shinkansen, opened in Japan in 1960. Since that time, similar trains, some able to travel at speeds of more than 300km/h, have entered service in other parts of Asia and Europe.

High-speed trains are all electric – obtaining their power from electrified rails below or from power cables running above the railway line. This electricity powers a series of electric motors to propel the train rapidly without it needing to carry heavy, bulky fuel such as diesel. At higher speeds, all vehicles face resistance from the air they pass through. The front of a high-speed train is designed to be streamlined so that it cuts through the air as smoothly as possible.

A TGV (*Train à Grande Vitesse*) high-speed train races through France, reaching a top speed of 320km/h at some points on its route. More than 2 billion passengers have been carried on France's high-speed rail system since it opened in 1981.

OVERHEAD POWER

A Pendolino tilting train tilts so that it can round curves in the track without slowing down. Many electric trains rely on power cables directly above the track to provide them with electricity.

Headlights and warning lights on the front of the train.

03

Steel track precisely made to help the train travel as smoothly as possible.

MAGLEV

Maglev (magnetic levitation) trains use powerful electromagnets that repel each other to lift the train above the track, called a guideway. Further electromagnets along the side of the guideway attract the train, pulling it forwards. The fastest Maglev trains travel at speeds of more than 400km/h.

Propulsion magnets along side of guideway propel train forward.

Guideway magnet repels train magnet.

Electromagnets repel each other, causing train to float above guideway.

Train driver in crash-protected cab monitors engine computers and signals.

Main transformer weighs 8 tonnes and converts the voltage down to 1,500 volts for the train's engine.

Pantograph receives 25,000 volts of electricity from the overhead power line.

Motor bogie uses two 1,000 horsepower electric motors to turn wheels.

HOW DO SUBMARINES DIVE?

Submarines are built so that they can float in water or dive below the surface. They do this by means of large ballast tanks that are wrapped around their hull (body). These can be filled with water or air in order to change the submarine's weight.

When a submarine's ballast tanks are filled with air, it is lighter in weight than the water it displaces (pushes out of its way) and so it rises upwards. To dive, the tanks are filled with water so that the submarine becomes heavier and sinks. Once the submarine reaches the desired depth, water is blown out of special ballast tanks, called negative tanks, to make the submarine weigh the same amount as the water it displaces. The submarine will then float under the water and can cruise along, changing direction using one or more flaps called rudders on its tail.

An Ohio Class submarine used by the US Navy is 170m long and can weigh more than 18,750 tonnes when submerged. Powered by a nuclear reactor, this giant sub can travel on missions lasting up to three months.

Radio and radar antennae

Periscope provides views from above the water when the sub is just below the surface.

Wing-like diving planes tilt up or down to help the submarine dive or rise.

Living quarters for the 155 officers and crew.

Inner pressure hull is 7.5cm thick, and strong enough to withstand high pressure.

Large sonar dome measures distances to objects ahead of the submarine.

Large buoyancy or ballast tanks are located between the outer hull and inner pressure hull.

Nuclear reactor (see pages 104–05) creates high pressure steam.

Steam-powered turbines turn the drive shaft.

Drive shaft connects turbine to propeller.

Large, seven-bladed propeller screw turns to push the submarine through the water.

SUBMERSIBLE

This DeepSee submersible is just 6m long, holds up to three people and can dive down to 450m. It uses large containers called bladders that it empties to dive and fills with air to surface.

GOING UP, GOING DOWN

A submarine uses large ballast tanks surrounding its interior to control its buoyancy. These tanks can be flooded with water to make the sub heavier so that it will sink. To surface, compressed air forces the water out of the tanks.

1. To surface, air is forced through the sub's tanks, pushing the water out. As air fills the tanks the submarine rises to the surface.

2. To dive, the sub's lower tank valves are opened. Water fills the tanks, making the submarine heavier and allowing it to descend.

HOW DO JET ENGINES WORK?

A jet engine is a type of internal combustion engine that generates thrust out of its rear exhaust to propel it forwards. Jet engines are found on many airliners and fast military aircraft and, occasionally, on record-breaking fast cars.

Cold air is drawn into the front of a jet engine and then squeezed by a series of turning turbine blades to increase its pressure and its temperature. The air then enters the combustion chamber where it is mixed with fuel and burned, reaching temperatures of about 900°C. Large amounts of hot gases are produced and expand out of the back of the combustion chamber and the rear exhaust nozzle. The force of these rapidly expanding gases creates an equal force in the opposite direction, thrusting the aircraft or land vehicle forwards.

Smooth engine covering is called a nacelle. The engines burn about 18 litres of fuel per second.

Large air 'intakes' channel air into the jet engine.

Nose cap

...... Parachutes to float the booster safely back to Earth.

SOLID-FUEL ROCKET
Some rocket engines are fuelled by a ready-mixed combination of solid fuel and oxidizer (an oxygen-producing substance). The two solid rocket boosters (SRBs) used on the former Space Shuttle carried about 500,000kg of fuel and provided over 80 per cent of the Shuttle's thrust at lift-off. Within two minutes, all of their fuel was used up.

...... Small motors fire up to remove SRB from Space Shuttle.

Igniter sets light to solid fuel and oxidizer mixture.

Long, tapering nose is designed to slice through the air and keep drag to a minimum.

Eurofighter Typhoon needs extra thrust as it takes off.

Glowing engine exhausts as afterburners operate.

AFTERBURNERS

Some jet engines, particularly those fitted to fast military jets, generate extra thrust using afterburners. These are parts of a jet engine that spray extra fuel into the exhaust gases to generate extra thrust.

High-pressure air and fuel ignite and burn in the combustion chamber.

Tail wing

Snug cockpit is accessed from a roof hatch.

Gases expand rapidly out of the rear of the jet engine.

Compression fan blades squeeze air, increasing its pressure.

ROCKET POWER

Rocket engines operate in space, where there is no air to mix with fuel as in a jet engine. Rocket engines must carry their own supply of oxidizer (oxygen-producing chemicals) in tanks. This is pumped with fuel into the combustion chamber and burned.

Thrust SSC is the world land speed record holder. In 1997, in the Black Rock Desert in Nevada, USA, the 16.5m-long single-seat vehicle raced to a speed of 1,228km/h. It was powered by two large jet engines, normally found in Phantom military jet aircraft.

Oxidizer tank

Combustion chamber

Nozzle

Fuel tank

Pump moves fuel into combustion chamber

119

HOW ARE THINGS LAUNCHED INTO SPACE?

A rocket's payload is the cargo it carries into space. This could be a space capsule containing astronauts or a communications satellite that will orbit Earth. Launching a payload into space requires vast amounts of thrust from rocket engines.

A launch vehicle's giant rocket engines need huge amounts of fuel and oxidizer. The five F1 engines on a *Saturn V*, for instance, used over 8,900kg of liquid oxygen and 3,940kg of fuel per second. Fuel, oxidizer and engines are extremely heavy to carry into space, so two methods are used, sometimes together. Booster rockets provide extra thrust at lift-off but then fall away once their fuel is used up, making the launch vehicle lighter and needing less thrust to power it. Some launch vehicles have two or three stages, each with their own rocket engines. Once a stage finishes powering the vehicle, it falls away to reduce the rocket's overall weight, and the next stage's engine fires and takes over.

Fregat has one main engine and 12 small thrusters that allow it to manoeuvre into precise position.

...............The second stage of the launch vehicle continues to rise using its own rocket engines.

This *Soyuz-Fregat* launch vehicle is built in three stages. In 2015, it will propel the *BepiColombo* space probe on its journey to Mercury. Over 1,700 *Soyuz* launch vehicles have lifted off from Earth since the first in 1967.

Four 19.8m-long booster rockets, each weighing 42 tonnes, are jettisoned once they have used up their fuel.................................

Once all of its fuel is used up, the second stage falls away and will burn up in the Earth's atmosphere.......................

TYPES OF ORBIT

Satellites can be put into different types of orbit around Earth or another body in space.

.... Elliptical orbit used for some navigation and communication satellites.

Low Earth orbit .... used for weather and spy satellites.

Polar orbit used for weather and land-imaging satellites.................

Geosynchronous orbit used for.......... communications and navigation.

Dish receives instructions and sends back data via radio waves to Earth.

Capsule contains space probe.

BepiColombo probe comprises two separate spacecraft – the Mercury Planetary Orbiter (MPO) and the Mercury Magnetospheric Orbiter (MMO).

LOOKING DOWN

Many satellites launched into space follow a circular or elliptical path as they orbit Earth. They perform a range of useful tasks, from tracking storms to taking satellite images of Earth (below).

ION THRUSTER

An alternative form of thrust can be provided by an ion thruster. This generates thrust by accelerating ions (electrically charged atoms or molecules). It is weaker than thrusters that use fuel and oxidizer, but lasts longer, and can propel vehicles to greater speeds.

121

HOW IS A SPACE STATION BUILT?

Space stations are large spacecraft that are designed to stay in space for a long period of time. They contain living quarters for crews of astronauts and have one or more docking ports so that other spacecraft can arrive and leave.

The first space stations, such as NASA's *Skylab* and the Soviet Union's *Salyut 1*, were single units built on Earth and carried into space by large launch vehicles. The *Mir* space station in the 1980s was the first to be constructed out of a number of separate modules, each sent into space via a separate launch vehicle. The construction of the International Space Station (ISS) began in 1998 and is the ultimate in modular design. Assembled over the course of more than 120 spaceflights, the space station consists of a long truss to which giant solar panels, modules, docking ports and nodes, which connect different parts of the station to each other, are all attached.

Two astronauts perform an extravehicular activity (a spacewalk) to complete tasks on the exterior of the ISS.

The ISS is .... 109m wide and on Earth would weigh more than 420,000kg.

LIVING IN SPACE
The ISS has been lived in continuously since 2000. Crews tend to spend 3–6 months on board before being swapped over via a docking spacecraft that may also bring new experiments, equipment, food and other supplies.

ROBOT ARM
Several different robotic arms have been used on the ISS to handle modules and parts. This Canadarm 2 robot arm handles the *HTV-2* – a Japanese unmanned spacecraft that carried supplies to the ISS and removed rubbish and materials no longer needed by the crew.

The ISS makes 15.7 orbits of Earth every day, at altitudes of between 330km and 410km.

Module fitted to the space station contains a laboratory and large numbers of space experiments.

PLSS (primary life support subsystem) backpack supplies oxygen to the astronaut and electrical power to the suit.

Helmet contains radio for communication with other astronauts.

123

....Crater is approximately 730m wide.

VIEW BELOW

Orbiting and fly-by space probes take many digital images of a body's surface from above. These are then relayed to Earth and examined by scientists. This image is from the Mars Reconnaissance Orbiter and shows an impact crater on Mars.

The *ExoMars* rover is a robot planned to arrive on Mars in 2016. It will navigate its own way around the planet's surface and use a drill and onboard mini chemistry lab to analyse samples of soil and rock to search for signs of present or past life forms.

......Twin cameras enable the rover to build up a 3D map of the ground ahead.

Solar panels power the robot by generating electricity from sunlight.

Antenna can send.............................. and receive data and instructions via radio waves.

Controller inside .... body helps plot the best route forwards for the rover, avoiding large obstacles.

Each wheel can be steered .... independently by the rover.

Drillbox able to drill holes ...... into the planet's surface, up to 2m deep.

HOW DO MACHINES EXPLORE PLANETS?

Space probes are unmanned machines that are sent into space to explore other planets in the Solar System, as well as moons, the Sun, asteroids and comets. They use radio signals to send back digital images and measurements made with scientific instruments.

Probes are launched from Earth by rocket-powered launch vehicles, and are sent on carefully calculated flight paths to their target. Their journeys may take many years. The *Cassini-Huygens* space probe took seven years to reach Saturn. Some probes fly by different planets or moons on the way to their main target. The *Voyager 2* probe, for example, performed fly-bys of Jupiter, Saturn, Uranus and Neptune. Other probes go into orbit around their target and may drop a separate lander probe onto a planet or a moon. Some lander probes stay in the one place while others are mobile rovers that can trundle across the surface and analyse the rock and soil using scientific instruments.

Large solar panels provide electricity to power the probe's equipment.

..... 3m-wide antenna sends images back to Earth.

High-resolution cameras .... can pick out other space probes operating on Mars's surface.

ORBITERS

Probes such as this Mars Reconnaissance Orbiter (MRO) go into orbit around their target. Their scientific instruments may measure the atmosphere, weather and surface. The MRO orbits Mars every 112 minutes and uses high-resolution cameras to photograph every part of the planet's surface.

TOUCHDOWN!

Getting a probe to reach the surface of a planet, comet or moon can be tricky and many probes have been lost on their descent. In 2005, the *Huygens* probe successfully landed on one of Saturn's moons, Titan, more than 1.2 billion km away from Earth. Beneath the haze of Titan's atmosphere, the probe discovered a world of dunes and rocks, with seas of liquid methane.

1. Heat shield protected probe as it travelled through Titan's thick atmosphere.

2. Parachute opened to slow down probe and the heat shield was jettisoned.

3. Probe gathered information about Titan's atmosphere and surface as it descended and for 90 minutes after it landed.

HOW WOULD A CREWED BASE ON THE MOON WORK?

It is more than 40 years since a human astronaut has set foot on the Moon, but many think that humans will return to the Moon in the future, possibly living in a dedicated base on its surface.

A permanent base on the Moon might allow scientists to build and operate radio telescopes and other scientific instruments free of the distortion and pollution of Earth's atmosphere. Unmanned reusable spacecraft could ferry supplies to the base regularly, taking less than three days to travel from Earth to the Moon. Their return journey, carrying back valuable materials mined or processed on the Moon, would use less power and fuel because the Moon's gravity is only about one-sixth of Earth's. This means that less thrust is required to lift off from the lunar surface and head home to Earth or on missions further afield to other parts of the Solar System.

Robotic servicer

Satellite

1. Unmanned space station contains fuel tanks to service docking spacecraft.

2. Satellite docks with station and is refuelled, repaired or dismantled.

REFUELLING
In the future, space stations may be built to refuel spacecraft on their journeys to and from the Moon or beyond. They will be fitted with docking ports for spacecraft to latch on to, while their tanks are filled with fuel. Satellites may also be captured and refuelled to extend their working lives.

.... The six-man 'crew' of the Mars-500 experiment emerge after 520 days.

MARS-500
Manned missions to Mars may involve a journey of up to 18 months, using the Moon as a launch platform. The Mars-500 experiment simulated living in a spacecraft-like environment to test the effects of a long space journey on humans.

:..... Moonbase built into the lunar surface, which helps to insulate the structures.

Large robot arm grips and................. moves rocks and other large objects.

A spacecraft takes off from the surface before heading back to Earth carrying minerals and experiments.

Spherical storage tanks hold rocket engine fuel.

Domed structure might provide living quarters for several dozen lunar workers.

Moon rover, powered by electric batteries, transports astronauts around the surface.

127

SCIENCE AND TECHNOLOGY
FIND OUT MORE ABOUT HOW THE WORLD WORKS

WEBSITES TO VISIT

www.smartplanet.com/videos/robots
Watch videos and reports on the latest robot explorers and mobile machines at the Smart Planet website.

http://science.howstuffworks.com/nanotechnology.htm
Learn more about nanotechnology at the How Stuff Works website.

www.darvill.clara.net/altenerg/nuclear.htm
Get lots of details about all sorts of energy sources, from nuclear power to wind power, at this informative website.

http://news.bbc.co.uk/1/shared/spl/hi/guides/456900/456932/html/default.stm
Read this brief guide to how nuclear power works, including a handy chart detailing the advantages and disadvantages of different energy sources.

www.pbs.org/wgbh/nova/bridge/
Learn how to survey land and select the right bridge type for different situations at these web pages presented by PBS.

www.navy.mil/navydata/cno/n87/faq.html
Read the answers to more than 60 frequently asked questions about submarines, published by the US Navy.

www.nasa.gov/audience/foreducators/topnav/materials/listbytype/How_Rockets_Work.html
Learn more about how rockets work using NASA's detailed Rockets Educator Guide.

www.thetech.org/exhibits/online/satellite/
Read about satellites, the orbits they are put into and their different jobs at this small but informative website.

www.spacekids.co.uk/spacesuits/
See how spacesuits for astronauts performing spacewalks have developed over time.

www.nasa.gov/mission_pages/station/main/index.html
Find out all you want to know about the International Space Station at NASA's detailed web pages on the giant orbiting satellite.

BOOKS TO LOOK OUT FOR

• BASHER SCIENCE: TECHNOLOGY by Basher and Dan Green (Kingfisher, 2012)
• NATURE GOT THERE FIRST by Phil Gates (Kingfisher, 2010)
• LEGENDARY JOURNEYS: SPACE by Dr Mike Goldsmith (Kingfisher, 2012)

CHAPTER FIVE
HISTORY

HOW WERE THE EARLIEST TOWNS FORMED?

About 10,000 years ago, peoples who had previously wandered and hunted for their food began to grow crops and domesticate animals. As they started settling in one place, villages developed, some of which would expand to become the first towns and cities.

As early peoples became more skilled at farming, they created surpluses of food that they began to trade with others. This need for markets saw some of the first settlements form close to the farmers' fields and often near rivers. As these settlements grew larger, services were established for the inhabitants to use, such as shops, water supplies and harbours for boats. Soon, some people developed other skills besides farming and became metalworkers and tool-makers. People also gathered together in early towns to defend themselves from other, hostile, groups. Some of these towns built protective surrounding walls.

Located on the banks of the River Euphrates in present-day Iraq, the city of Ur was founded almost 6,000 years ago. A settlement of the Sumerian civilization, it featured public buildings, including temples and markets with houses on its outskirts.

TOWN ON STILTS

In the third millennium BCE, while the Egyptians were building pyramids, the Celtic people of Europe lived in fortified villages. Many were on river banks where they could easily be defended. The wooden houses were surrounded by a high stockade.

Thatched, straw roofs with a gap to let out the smoke.

Houses built on stilts to protect against seasonal floods.

Pathways made of split logs.

Temple walls made of mud bricks and measuring approximately 45m wide and 65m long.

The Ziggurat of Ur, dedicated to the moon god, Nanna, is the largest temple in the city.

MOHENJO-DARO
The ruins of this ancient city, located in the Indus Valley of Pakistan, were rediscovered in 1921. At its peak, as many as 35,000 people may have lived in the city, making it one of the largest ancient cities in the world.

A religious ceremony is performed inside the temple walls.

People buy animals, food and goods to trade in the town market.

Oxen used to pull simple wooden carts.

HOW WERE MUMMIES MADE?

Mummies are bodies that have been preserved so they do not decay. Many civilizations created mummies, including the Egyptians. They believed that preserving a body after death would allow the soul to survive in the afterlife. Some Egyptian mummies have survived intact for more than 5,000 years.

Rituals surrounded all stages of mummification. The process began with washing the body. Key organs were then removed and preserved before being placed in special ceremonial containers called canopic jars. The heart was left inside the body because the Egyptians believed it would be weighed in the afterlife to determine whether the person had led a good life. After being packed with salts and left on a table to dry out, the body would be washed again, covered in oils and artificial eyes would be added to the head. Once the mummy was complete, the funeral ceremony could be held.

COFFINS

This shows the mummy of an Egyptian queen, complete with a painted death mask, being placed inside an elaborate coffin. A priest would recite spells from the Book of the Dead to protect the queen on her journey to the afterlife.

Coffin was made from cartonnage, a mix of plaster and papyrus, as wood was scarce.

PREPARING A MUMMY

The mummification process took about 70 days. For 40 days the body was left to dry after being packed with natron salt crystals. The salt absorbed the moisture from the body and prevented it from rotting. Only when the body was dry could the wrapping process begin.

1. Body is washed and purified with palm wine.

2. Stomach is removed, followed by the lungs, intestines and liver.

3. A hook inserted up the nostrils is used to scrape out the brain.

4. Body is washed free of natron salt and then oiled.

5. Body is stuffed with leaves, linen and sawdust.

Embalmers work to mummify an Egyptian king in an embalming tent close to the site of his tomb. They wrap the body in layers of linen bandages and use resin from trees to stick the linen wrappings together.

ANIMAL MUMMIES

The ancient Egyptians mummified dead animals, too, and left them in temples as offerings to the gods. Archaeologists have found mummies of pet cats as well as ibis birds and even crocodiles.

Outer layers of linen wrapped .... horizontally and vertically to form an elaborate pattern.

Priest reads chants and prayers from a papyrus scroll.

Body is covered in oils and perfumes.

Priest in charge of the embalming wears the jackal head of Anubis, god of mummification and the afterlife.

Amulets, thought to protect the body with magic, are slipped between the bandages.

HOW DID EGYPTIANS WRITE?

The ancient Egyptians recorded much information about their daily lives – from the details of harvests and taxes, to letters, royal orders and prayers. Over time, they developed a number of different scripts. The most famous was the hieroglyphic script, a form of picture-writing developed more than 5,000 years ago.

Hieroglyphs used images to represent objects and, later, certain sounds, so that information could be written down, stored and communicated. This work was done by trained scribes. Scribes supervised the carving of hieroglyphs into stone, but they themselves mostly wrote on pieces of pottery called ostraca, or on papyrus. This was made from the flattened strips of marsh reeds, pressed and dried to form long sheets. A scribe would write with a brush of frayed river reeds, dipped in an ink made from soot or rocky minerals ground down and mixed with liquid.

The Great Temple of Amun at Karnak was an enormous ceremonial centre on the banks of the Nile. It was altered and expanded over many centuries by some 30 different pharaohs. Its pillars and walls were richly decorated in hieroglyphs.

A pharaoh's name is written inside an oval frame called a cartouche. ....

Outer rind of the papyrus stem is peeled away.	Inner pith is cut into strips and laid out in a layer.	A second, horizontal layer is flattened over the first and dried.

PAPYRUS

The reed's fibres made the papyrus scroll stronger than paper, and many scrolls have survived. This triangular-stemmed plant grew in abundance along the River Nile, and was used to make boats, baskets, sandals and writing material.

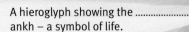

A hieroglyph showing the .... ankh – a symbol of life.

HIEROGLYPHS

Hieroglyphs were used for more than 3,000 years before they fell into disuse. It was only in the 19th century that the meaning of the different characters, numbering more than 2,000, was deciphered.

The pylon, or gateway, into the main hall of the temple.

Hieroglyphs carved into stone pillars and painted in bright colours.

HOW WERE PYRAMIDS BUILT?

A pyramid is a structure with four triangular sides sloping inwards to a point. A number of civilizations built pyramids as religious temples. The most famous pyramids are those built by the ancient Egyptians as tombs for their pharaohs (kings).

Of the 100 or so pyramid ruins in Egypt, the Great Pyramid at Giza is the largest. It was built for the pharaoh Khufu in about 2500BCE and consists of as many as 2.3 million large, limestone blocks. All of these blocks had to be cut precisely, smoothed and then moved into position – an enormous feat of organization. As many as 25,000–30,000 men worked on the construction, some permanently employed by the pharaoh, with thousands more farmworkers joining them for a few months each year when the Nile flooded and they could not work their fields.

This sprawling settlement was where the thousands of pyramid builders lived during the 20 or more years it took to build Khufu's pyramid at Giza, 4,500 years ago. When completed, the pyramid stood 146.5m high and was the tallest building in the world for more than 3,000 years.

Granary stored grain for use by bakers to make the thousands of loaves of bread needed every day.

STEPS

The first pyramids in Egypt were built in a series of steps. In later reigns, the pharaohs added smooth sides, possibly to depict the rays of the Sun. The Great Pyramid was built with amazing geometrical accuracy, with its four sides lined up with true north, south, east and west.

1. As each block was placed, the Great Pyramid rose in steps, in a style similar to the first pyramid, known as the Step Pyramid.

2. The pyramid was covered in a smooth white limestone casing.

A cross-section reveals the complex of passages and chambers. Khufu was probably buried in the upper chamber. The chamber deep in the bedrock may have been built to mislead tomb robbers.

King's chamber

False chamber

Houses are made from mud and straw bricks and have flat roofs. The roof was also part of the home's living space.

A physician's house. Archaeologists have found evidence of broken bones that had been treated and healed.

RAMPS

The ancient Egyptians did not possess cranes or rope block and tackles, so they probably lifted the large stone blocks into place by dragging them up large ramps and then shifting them into place using levers made of wood or bronze.

Row of workers fitting stone blocks into the pyramid face.

Ramp may have been made of rocks and packed-down earth.

Water-carrying channel is lined with smooth cement.

ROMAN ROADS

Roman roads were built as straight as possible to provide the shortest route between locations – vital for their marching legions. Roads consisted of a number of layers and had a camber – a curved surface higher in the middle than at the edges – to drain off rainwater.

1. After a surveyor had marked the ground, a trench was dug and lined with large stones and then smaller stones.

2. A layer of concrete was then rammed firmly into place by hand. The top layer was made of close-fitting paving slabs.

Wooden framework helps to support a newly built arch while construction is underway.

HOW DID THE ROMANS BUILD?

The Romans were resourceful engineers. They built great networks of roads and many bridges, the largest of which, the Trajan Bridge, spanned the River Danube and was more than 1km long.

Roman engineers planned major building works carefully before the teams of workers began baking bricks, quarrying stone, cutting wood and mixing cement. The Romans were great innovators and developed strong concrete made from pozzolana (volcanic ash), lime mortar and gravel. This was used in many of their structures, including about 80,000km of roads throughout the Roman Empire. They also adopted innovations from other peoples, such as the arch, first developed by the Etruscans (an early Italian civilization), which the Romans used in bridges, aqueducts and tunnels.

An aqueduct is built to convey a constant supply of clean water from higher ground to a Roman settlement. The Romans used basic machines such as the lever and pulley, as well as cranes, to build their structures.

Stones already cut to fit the arch are lowered using a polyspastos treadwheel crane.

POLYSPASTOS CRANE
The Romans built a range of different cranes to lift and lower building materials. This polyspastos crane featured a large treadwheel instead of a hand-turned winch. As a result, it could lift greater weights of up to 6,000kg.

1. Two or four men climbed into the large treadwheel and began to turn it by walking and pushing.

2. As the large wheel turned, it pulled ropes that lifted the crane's arm, and its load, upwards.

ROMAN AQUEDUCT
The Pont du Gard is part of a 50km-long Roman aqueduct, a structure built to transport water to the Roman settlement at Nîmes, France. Constructed of three layers of stone arches, it stands 49m high and is 275m long.

The aqueduct could transport as much as 200 million litres of water per day.

HOW DID ROMANS LIVE IN TOWNS?

The Romans built new towns throughout their empire, a large number of which had a similar layout. Most featured a grid of streets interconnecting at right angles with public facilities such as markets, temples, baths and bakeries.

Wealthy Romans lived in private houses, but most townspeople lived in single- or two-roomed *cenacula*. These were small flats inside apartment buildings that were often built close together on narrow streets. Running water was rare, so most Romans used public lavatories, collected water from public fountains and visited Roman baths. At the centre of a Roman town was a large square known as a forum. This was where the government offices and law courts were situated, but it was also a place for people to meet, do business and shop.

A shipment of slaves is offered for sale by auction.

PRIVATE HOME

A wealthy Roman's townhouse had a windowless outer wall and a large *atrium* (living room) with a hole in its sloping roof. This fed rainwater into a pool for drinking and washing.

Rooms looked onto an inner courtyard with a garden.

The *triclinium* was the dining room, with low couches to lie on while eating.

Kitchen called a *culina* where slaves prepared food.

A residential area in a large Roman town had its own small markets and meeting places away from the central forum. Poorer Romans lived in small apartments in *insulae* buildings, many of which were made of wood and posed a fire risk.

Open-air hot food stalls sell meals to the many town dwellers whose homes do not have kitchens.

Craftsmen and farmers sell their goods at a local market.

HYPOCAUST

Some homes of the rich and noble, both in the city and in country villas, benefitted from a central heating system called a hypocaust, which channelled warm air around the rooms.

A furnace generated heat that travelled through a basement created by raising the floor on a series of columns called piers.

Piers made of bricks or concrete.

An important Roman travels through the town in a 'litter' carried by slaves.

HOW WERE CASTLES BESIEGED?

Siege! An invading army is on the march. People have fled to the one local stronghold, an imposing stone castle. Within its stout walls may be stores of food and water, but can those inside hold out against a fierce army outside?

Many armies aimed not to destroy a castle but to capture it. Some would set up camp and secure nearby farms to feed their troops while stopping food from going in and messages from coming out. Eventually, the starving occupants would surrender. Other forces would try to tunnel under a castle's walls or use deception to gain entry. To try to shorten a long siege, archers fired volleys of arrows, some lit with burning tar, into a castle. Siege weapons such as the trebuchet and the mangonel rained down missiles. Often, a siege ended with a bloody storming of the castle gates and walls to get inside.

Chateau Gaillard (below) was built in northern France by English King Richard I to withstand any attack. But in 1203–04, the French armies of Phillip II laid siege to the castle, battered its walls and stormed into it. The siege lasted for eight months.

Siege tower, or belfry

SIEGE TOWER
This wheeled tower was rolled up to a castle's walls. A mini drawbridge was lowered onto the ramparts. Attackers then tried to cross the bridge into the castle.

Wood or animal-hide armour, sometimes coated in mud or soaked in vinegar to resist fire

Spring-loaded mangonel catapult hurls flaming missiles and rocks.

TREBUCHET

This ingenious, catapult-like machine could hurl rocks weighing as much as two men in an arc up and over castle walls.

1. Early trebuchets were powered by people, but later models used a huge rock as a counterweight. When dropped, the weight flung a long arm upwards. At the end of the arm was the weapon load, often held in a sling.

2. As the arm came over, the sling hurled the weapon at its target. Sometimes, trebuchets were loaded with rotting, dead animals to spread disease.

Weapon load flies away with great force.

Counterweight

......Sling

BATTERING RAM

This large, iron-tipped tree trunk, hanging on chains inside a wooden structure, was swung back and forth against castle gates.

Roof protected........................
attackers from
arrows and stones.

HOW DID THE BLACK DEATH SPREAD?

The Black Death was a devastating epidemic of the bubonic plague virus that swept through Europe and the Middle East during the 14th century. It caused the deaths of many millions of people.

Bubonic plague is a disease caused by the *Yersinia pestis* bacteria, which are mostly carried by infected fleas. The fleas infest the bodies of rats, and as the rats die from the disease, the fleas, searching for food, infect humans. An outbreak of the plague may have occurred in China in the 1340s and spread to the Mediterranean, carried over sea by ships and overland by traders along common trade routes. The disease spread quickly, helped by the fact that no one knew how to treat or cure it, and by the unclean living conditions of medieval towns, where food and toilet waste were often thrown onto the streets.

People bring out their dead at night from the homes of a plague-ridden town. The populations of some cities, such as Paris and Hamburg, were halved by the Black Death, while those living in many small towns and villages were wiped out completely.

A plague doctor carries a lantern and wears heavy robes and a beaked mask. The cone of the mask was filled with straw, herbs and scents, which were thought to ward off the plague.

SPREADING QUICKLY

These maps show how quickly the disease spread throughout much of Europe, reaching Russia and Britain, where some 1.5 million out of a total population of 4 million died.

1347

1348

1349

1353

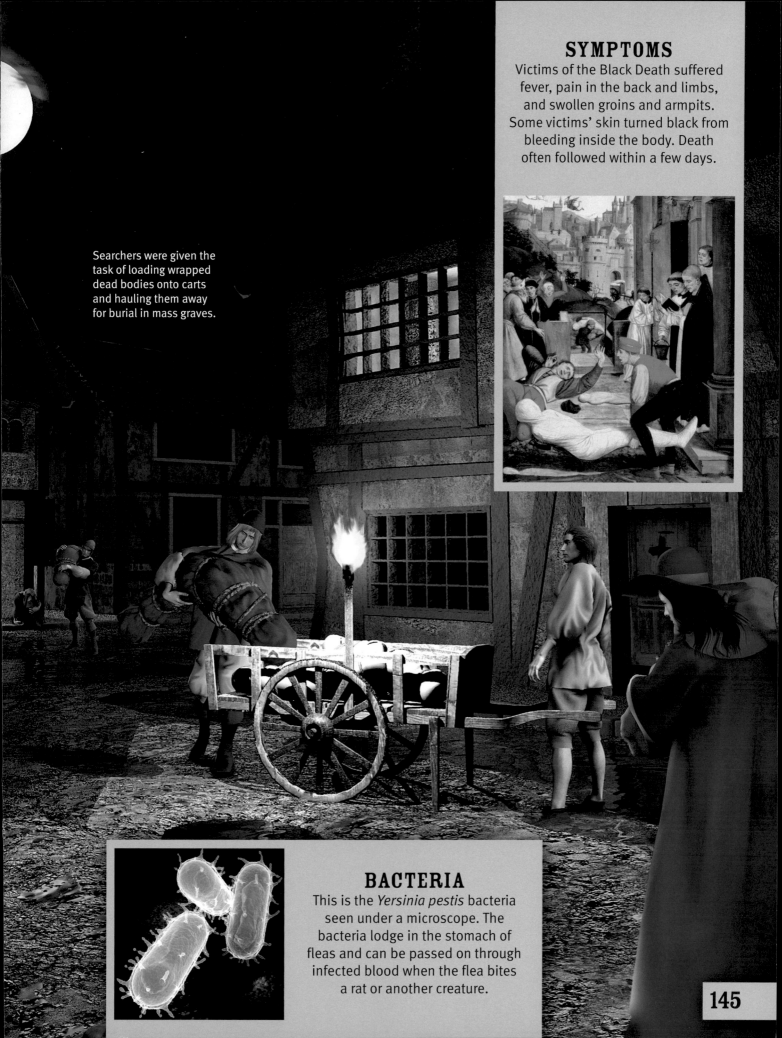

Searchers were given the task of loading wrapped dead bodies onto carts and hauling them away for burial in mass graves.

SYMPTOMS

Victims of the Black Death suffered fever, pain in the back and limbs, and swollen groins and armpits. Some victims' skin turned black from bleeding inside the body. Death often followed within a few days.

BACTERIA

This is the *Yersinia pestis* bacteria seen under a microscope. The bacteria lodge in the stomach of fleas and can be passed on through infected blood when the flea bites a rat or another creature.

HOW DID THE INCAS BUILD AN EMPIRE?

The Inca civilization emerged in the highlands of Peru in the 13th century and flourished for more than 200 years along South America's mountainous western coast. In the 1530s its supremacy came to an end with the arrival of the Spanish conquistadors.

The Incas began expanding their territory suddenly in the 1400s under the rulers Pachacutec and, later, Túpac Yupanqui. Every male Inca had to serve in the army and their sheer numbers overwhelmed enemies in battle. Historians also believe that the Incas used diplomacy and bargaining to extend their empire in places. The Incas were excellent engineers, using local materials to create terraced (stepped) farmlands from mountain slopes and to channel rivers for irrigation. They built about 40,000km of trails or roads that enabled their armies and convoys of llamas carrying food and goods to travel quickly. Foot messengers were staged at posts along many roads to create a communications system.

INCA EMPIRE

At its height in the 1520s, the Inca empire stretched from present-day Ecuador, south through Bolivia and Peru into central Chile and the borders of Argentina. It covered an area of 2 million square kilometres.

Atlantic Ocean

South America

Machu Picchu

Cusco, capital of the empire

Pacific Ocean

Granite blocks are quarried from 20km away; the heaviest weigh 100 tonnes.

ROPE BRIDGE

This suspension rope bridge allowed the Incas to cross the deep gorge cut by the River Apurímac in Peru. The Incas were skilled at making ropes out of twisted, woven plant fibres and built rope bridges as part of their road system.

Local Inca villagers had to keep bridges in good repair as part of their service to the empire.

FARMING

In steep mountain regions, the Incas cut steps into the slopes and built walls to form level terraces. On these they planted crops such as sweet potatoes and maize. They also channelled mountain streams to help water these narrow farm fields.

.............................Soil shored up by stone walls.

Construction of the giant Inca fortress of Sacsayhuamán was almost complete by the 15th century. This enormous stone fortress built on the edge of the Inca capital at Cusco, in present-day Peru, features walls up to 400m long made of giant, dry rocks.

Each stone is cut carefully using hand chisels so that it fits into the wall without the need for cement or mortar.............................

....................The Incas have not invented the wheel, so stones are dragged using stout ropes pulled by many people.

BOARDING

Here, pirates use a small boat to board a merchant ship. Hooked grappling irons tied to ropes are thrown and snag on the ship's rail, allowing the pirates to climb aboard and fight to take control.

Pirates were often armed with short, curved swords – good for close fighting.

Fierce hand-to-hand fighting breaks out on deck.

Pirates climb ropes up onto ship's deck.

HOW DID PIRATES CAPTURE TREASURE?

Piracy means attacking and robbing ships at sea. It has a long history, but the 16th, 17th and 18th centuries were the golden age of piracy. This was a time when galleons laden with gold crossed the Caribbean Sea, and celebrated pirates sought to rob them.

Merchant ships often carried valuable cargoes of gold, silver and spices. Pirates in the golden age would cruise the shipping routes or lurk in quiet bays waiting to ambush such ships for their treasure, or even to capture the ship for themselves. Sometimes, a pirate might use his notoriety, sailing very close and hoisting his flag to intimidate the other ship. Pirates might also fire cannon shots over the ship to force its surrender. On other occasions, they would bring their own ship alongside or use small boats to board and take over the ship and capture its valuable cargo.

Main sail catches wind to propel the 30m-long ship at high speed across the sea.

Blackbeard's flag showed a devil spearing a heart dripping blood.

Heavy cannon takes four men to operate and fires shot, each weighing 10kg.

Queen Anne's Revenge was the flagship of the notorious 18th-century pirate Edward Teach, known as Blackbeard. The ship had been captured by another pirate who gave it to Teach. He used it to attack and plunder more than a dozen ships in the Caribbean region and off the east coast of North America.

CANNONS

Cannons were the most powerful weapons on a ship. They used a charge of explosive, usually gunpowder, to fire a large, heavy ball – known as a shot – with great force. A 10kg shot fired from a range of 90m could crash through timber a metre thick.

Gunpowder.............

Wadding.............

Muzzle

Ball

Blackbeard's own living quarters are at the front (bow) of the ship and are easier to defend if attacked.

Deep hull offers plenty of storage room for food, water, captured goods and treasure.

HOW DID CAPTAIN COOK REACH AUSTRALIA?

In 1768, Captain James Cook and 93 crew members sailed from Plymouth, England, on a three-year-long, round-the-world voyage of discovery on board the *Endeavour*.

Cook's orders were to sail to Tahiti, from where he was to search for a mysterious southern continent in the Pacific Ocean. A number of mariners had spotted parts of Australia or New Zealand but Cook was the first to reach both and accurately chart parts of their coastlines. He was an accomplished sailor and navigator who prepared for the journey carefully, equipped with a tough ship suitable for exploration. He also looked after his crew. Many sailors of the time suffered from scurvy and other diseases caused by unclean living conditions and a lack of fresh foods. Cook insisted that his crew keep as clean as possible and eat fresh food whenever they could to ward off disease.

COOK'S ROUTE

Cook's first voyage took him across the Atlantic, around Cape Horn and into the Pacific Ocean to Tahiti. From there he set off to explore New Zealand and Australia. Cook stopped in Indonesia for repairs and returned home in 1771.

1. Sextant is pointed towards the horizon (where sea and sky appear to meet). A swinging post – the index bar – can be moved along a curving scale marked with angles.

Index bar

Telescope

2. As the index bar is moved, the image through the telescope splits in two and the Sun is brought down to the horizon. The angle can be read off the curved scale and converted into the altitude of the Sun above the horizon.

Curved scale

SEXTANT AND NAVIGATION

Captain Cook used an instrument called a sextant to calculate the angle of the Sun or stars above the horizon. The angle was used with tables of star positions to calculate the ship's position.

HMS *Endeavour* is a former coal-carrying ship converted for the expedition. This 32m-long vessel is sturdily built and loaded with provisions and medical supplies for the long journey.

Over 2,700 square metres of sails allowed the ship to catch winds and travel fast.

Cook landed at Botany Bay, New South Wales, Australia, in 1770. He promptly claimed the land for the British crown.

LANDFALL

In 1769, Cook landed in New Zealand and met resistance from the Maori, whom he was forced to fight off. From there he sailed west to Australia, landing at Botany Bay, named after the large number of new plants found there.

Hull is surrounded with a double layer of planking to protect the vessel against rocks and wood-eating worms.

Stored provisions include 10,000 cuts of beef and pork, bread and barrels of pickled cabbage.

Broad, flat bottom allows the ship to sail well in shallow waters and to land on shores for repairs.

ENGINEERING

Other innovations of the Industrial Revolution included the use of blast furnaces to increase iron production for engines and railways. In 1779, the first cast-iron arch bridge was built – the Iron Bridge, over the River Severn in England.

Gases from coal burning in factories escape through tall chimneys.

Large textiles factories boomed in the northwest of England in the late 18th and 19th centuries. Many thousands of people moved from the countryside to towns to work in these factories.

Workers' cottages built in streets close to the factory.

RAILWAYS

Steam-powered locomotives were first used to haul coal during the Industrial Revolution. From 1830, the *Rocket*, invented by Robert Stephenson, was one of the first to haul passengers on services between the cities of Liverpool and Manchester.

Chimney

Boiler where water is heated into steam

Water to supply boiler

Barges and other shipping travelling along canals carry materials to and goods away from factories.

HOW DID STEAM POWER THE INDUSTRIAL REVOLUTION?

The Industrial Revolution began in Britain in the 18th century and soon spread to Western Europe and the United States. It saw the growth of large factories, producing vast quantities of materials or goods, using steam-powered machines.

The first steam engines were developed by English inventors – Thomas Savery in 1698 and Thomas Newcomen in 1712. At first, steam engines were put to work pumping water out of mines. It took the genius of Scottish inventor James Watt and others in the 1760s onwards to create sophisticated steam engines capable of powering machines in factories. Later, larger steam engines were powering the ships and trains transporting goods and materials to and from the factories.

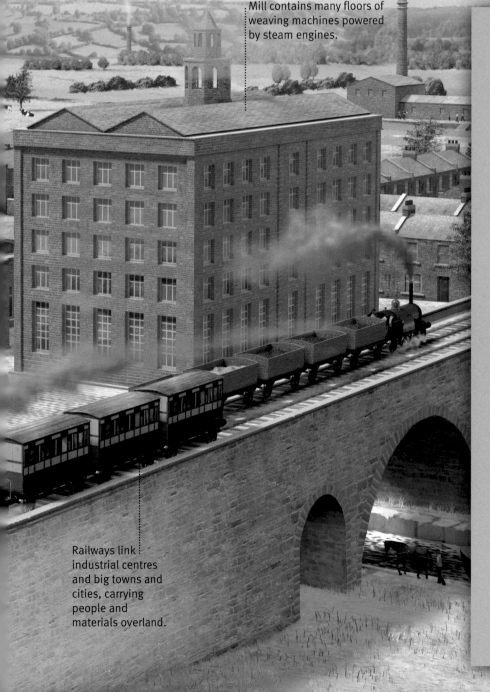

Mill contains many floors of weaving machines powered by steam engines.

Railways link industrial centres and big towns and cities, carrying people and materials overland.

STEAM ENGINE

In factories, steam engines were used to power giant flywheels. Belts turned by the flywheel would transfer power to the many spinning machines in a textiles mill, for example.

High-pressure steam pushes piston.

Steam escapes from valve.

Flywheel

1. Coal is used as fuel, which is burned in the furnace. The furnace heats the water in the tubes around the boiler.

Piston

Cylinder

2. The water turns to steam that, under pressure, enters a cylinder in which it pushes a rod called a piston.

Crankshaft

3. The back-and-forth movement of the piston is turned into a turning motion by a crankshaft.

SCIENCE AND TECHNOLOGY
FIND OUT MORE ABOUT HOW THE WORLD WORKS

WEBSITES TO VISIT

www.ancientegypt.co.uk/menu.html
Check out the lives of the ancient Egyptians at these web pages hosted by the famous British Museum in London.

www.eyelid.co.uk/hiromenu.htm
Find out how to write your name using hieroglyphs and more at these web pages dedicated to ancient Egypt.

www.roman-empire.net/
Learn how the Romans lived, how their empire expanded and much more on this large, detailed website with long, scrolling web pages.

http://science.howstuffworks.com/engineering/structural/10-roman-engineering-tricks.htm
Find out about construction techniques that the ancient Romans used or developed, and that we still use today.

www.castles-of-britain.com/castlelearningcenter.htm
A fascinating, in-depth guide to building, defending and living in castles, focused on the castles of Britain.

www.bbc.co.uk/history/british/middle_ages/black_01.shtml
Read accounts of what it was like to face the plague as it spread through the British Isles.

www.rmg.co.uk/explore/sea-and-ships/pirates/
Listen to podcasts about pirates and read up on pirate myths and facts at the UK's National Maritime Museum website.

www.bbc.co.uk/history/interactive/animations/navigation/index_embed.shtml
Follow the history of navigation at sea using this helpful series of animated web pages.

www.sl.nsw.gov.au/discover_collections/history_nation/voyages/discovery/index.html
View images from the journals of scientists and artists who travelled on Captain James Cook's voyages of exploration to the Pacific.

www.animatedengines.com/
Watch animations of different types of steam engines in action, and read more about how the different parts work together.

BOOKS TO LOOK OUT FOR

• THE CHILDREN'S ATLAS OF WORLD HISTORY by Simon Adams (Kingfisher, 2008)
• THE KINGFISHER GEOGRAPHY ENCYCLOPEDIA by Clive Gifford (Kingfisher, 2011)
• PLAGUES, POX AND PESTILENCE by Richard Platt (Kingfisher, 2011)
• THE KINGFISHER HISTORY ENCYCLOPEDIA by various authors (Kingfisher, 2012)

INDEX

ACKNOWLEDGEMENTS

The Publisher would like to thank the following for permission to reproduce their material. Every care has been taken to trace copyright holders. However, if there have been unintentional omissions or failure to trace copyright holders, we apologize and will, if informed, endeavour to make corrections in any future edition.

Top = t; Bottom = b; Centre = c; Left = l; Right = r

Cover Shutterstock/Four Oaks and pages 9 Getty/All Canada Photos; 12-13 Getty/Francois Lochon; 14 Shutterstock/Claudio Rossol; 17 Shutterstock/Terry W Ryder; 21 NASA/JPL; 22 Shutterstock/John A Anderson; 23 Shutterstock/deb22; 25tl Shutterstock/Chantal de Bruijne; 25tc Shutterstock/Chantal de Bruijne; 25tr Shutterstock/Israel Hervas Bengochea; 27 Shutterstock/Danshutter; 38 Dean Steadman/Kingfisher; 39 Science Photo Library/pascal goetheluck; 40 41 Shutterstock/Morphart Creation; 41 Shutterstock/Morphart Creation; 43 Alamy/Thomas Cockrem; 53 Shutterstock/Marques; 54 Shutterstock/leonello calvetti; 63 Shutterstock/Catmando; 79 Shutterstock/MCarter; 81 Shutterstock/Nadezhda Bolotina; 83c J Garden/Alamy; 86 Shutterstock/Susan Flashman; 89 Shutterstock/John Carnemolla; 93 Shutterstock/thelefty; 99t Shutterstock/Patricia Malina; 99b Getty/Tony Parker; 100 Getty Images/Liaison Agency; 101 U.S. Air Force Image Library; 103l Shutterstock/any-keen; 130r Getty/Yoshikazu Tsuno; 103br Shutterstock/Tyler Boyes; 105 Shutterstock/Andrea Danti; 106 Shutterstock/Toa55; 109 Getty/Peter Arnold; 110t Shutterstock/ Shalith; 110b Shutterstock/ Matej Hudovernik; 111 Shutterstock/Dan Breckwoldt; 112 Getty Images/Bloomberg; 113 Getty/David McNew; 115 Science Photo Library/Martin Bond; 117 Getty/Peter Arnold; 119 Shutterstock/Martijn Smeets; 120 Shutterstock/Anton Balazh; 122c Getty Images/Universal Images Group; 122b Getty Images/Stocktrek Images; 124 Time Life Pictures/Getty Images; 125 Getty Images/Universal Images Group; 126 Getty/AFP; 131 Getty Images/Ursula Gahwiler; 139 Shutterstock/StevanZZ; 145t Getty/BAL; 145b Shutterstock/Michael Taylor; 146 Getty Images/Glowimages; 147 Shutterstock/Neale Cousland; 151 Getty Images/Hulton Archive; 152tl Getty/Getty Images; 152b Getty/SSPL.

Extra art supplied by Roger Stewart.